DIVINE PURPOSE LIVING

DIVINE PURPOSE LIVING

Daily Nuggets
of
Wisdom and Inspiration

Dr. Andrew Robinson
Wanda Kay Robinson

Nearly all Scriptures taken from the Augmented King James Version Bible and a few from the King James Version Bible.

Published by Christ Ministries Inc.
Charleston, Illinois 61920
ChristMinistriesInc.org
ActsChristMinistries@gmail.com

ISBN: 9798739685148

Table of Contents

Day 1 Forgive the Unforgiveable

Now therefore fear not: I will nourish you, and your little ones. And he comforted them, and spoke kindly unto them.

Genesis 50:21

In Genesis 25 and 27, Jacob deceived his way into obtaining his elder brother Esau's birthright and blessing. Esau began to hate Jacob to the degree that he wanted Jacob dead, leaving the brothers alienated from one another for many years. They finally meet again in Genesis 33, where Jacob tells his brother, "I have seen your face, as though I had seen the face of God, and you were pleased with me," and surprisingly all is forgiven.

We can change people's opinion of us with kindness. God does not want us to live our lives vengeful in getting back at those who hurt us. Living with bitterness and anger only hinders us from a successful and joyful life. Let us demonstrate kindness to others that do not deserve it. May we be forgiving and merciful to anyone who has wronged us.

Being a Christian means to forgive the unforgivable, because Jesus has forgiven the unforgivable in us. Forgiveness is the saving of the heart. Forgiveness spares the cost of anger, the expense of hatred, the price of souls.

Day 2 Plan for Rest and Self-care

He makes me to lie down in green pastures: he leads me beside the still waters.

Psalm 23:2

A phrase that most likely describes each of us is "constantly busy." When our mind thinks always of business or problems to solve or if we work all the time, we become insipid and eventually burn out.

Jesus wants us to take time to rest our minds and our bodies. He even provided a Sabbath day so we could rest (see Exodus 20:8). If we do not take the time to replenish our minds and recharge our bodies, the Lord will "make us to lie down," because we will reach the stage where we cannot go on and we have to rest.

We need to be productive, yet balance our lives spiritually, emotionally, and physically. These should include with them rest, recreation, and fun. As important as it is to have a plan for being productive in our work, it is equally important to have a plan for rest and self-care.

May we trust that Jesus will lead us to what we need as we mature in having more and more of His righteous character. Ask Him to forgive us for getting too busy to hear His voice and to respond to His loving grace.

Day 3 A Second Touch

And he took the blind man by the hand, and led him out of the town; and when he had spit on his eyes, and put his hands upon him, he asked him if he saw ought. And he looked up, and said, see men as trees, walking. After that he put his hands again upon his eyes, and made him look up: and he was restored, and saw every man clearly.

Mark 8:23-25

The blind man probably would have been delighted and satisfied with simply seeing for the first time, even though everything was out of focus. The blurry vision could have been all he received at that time, but Jesus wanted complete healing for the man. So, He touched the blind man's eyes again, and they were completely healed.

Jesus is dissatisfied with mediocrity. Too often, we settle for less than His best for us. Our God desires to give us a second touch. May we always be grateful for what He has done, but keep our faith strong in trusting for the fulness of all that we are believing Him for.

What Jesus has started He will finish, if we will keep believing in His promise. Hold on! "You ain't seen nothing yet!"

Day 4 A Child of the King

And has made us unto our God kings and priests: and we shall reign on the earth.

Revelation 5:10

Jesus has made us kings and priests unto Him! The Lord desires for us to carry ourselves with confident expectation, knowing that we are royalty in Him. This does not mean for us to be conceited, but humbled and grateful that God has appointed us.

When we begin seeing ourselves as kings and priests in Him, we will never feel intimidated or inferior again. The King of kings and Lord of lords has crowned us with righteousness, glory, rejoicing and life (2 Timothy 4:8; 1 Peter 5:4; 1 Thessalonians 2:19; Revelation 2:10). Royalty is our identity. Servanthood is our mission. Intimacy with God is our source of empowerment and life. Royalty resides not in vain spectacle nor pride, but in great virtues and character.

Oh yes, oh yes, I'm a child of the King,

His royal Blood now flows through my veins,

And I, who was wretched and poor, now can sing,

Praise God! Praise God! I'm a child of the King!

Day 5 God Sees Our Heart

...For the Lord sees not as man sees; for man looks on the outward appearance, but the Lord looks on the heart.

I Samuel 16:7

When the prophet Samuel came looking for a king, David was ignored and considered insignificant by his family. They looked on the outside and saw a young, scrawny boy, but God saw the heart of a king.

People may ignore, exclude, or even judge a child of God based on the outward appearance, abilities, or skin color. But, Jesus does not. He looks on the inside of us. He sees our commitment, honesty, and integrity. If we continue to reverence and honor the Lord, He will move us from the back to the front, from last to first, and from least to greatest, just as He did for David.

People may try to hold us down, but Jesus will raise us up. Others do not define us or control our destiny...GOD DOES!

Day 6 Let the Redeemed Say So

Let the redeemed of the Lord say so, whom he has redeemed from the hand of the enemy.

Psalm 107:2

As children of God, we can give life to what we say. Our words can have creative power. God does not want us to simply "hope so" or "think so," He wants us to "say so!" If we speak negative things, we invite them into our life, but speaking positively brings blessings to us. In order to rise to the next level, we must proclaim victory in Jesus name. He spoke the world into existence. We should declare today that we will get the job we want, receive the promotion, achieve our goals, have healthy relationships with friends and family, and be victorious over spiritual strongholds.

To have success, to have wisdom, and to be prosperous and healthy, we need to do more than think and hope. Let us confidently proclaim words of faith and victory over ourselves and our families today in Jesus name!

Day 7 Turning Our Mess into a Miracle

And David comforted Bathsheba his wife, and went in unto her, and lay with her: and she bare a son, and he called his name Solomon: and the Lord loved him.

I Samuel 12:24

David had sinned terribly by having Uriah killed and by taking the man's wife, Bathsheba, for his own wife. After being rebuked by the prophet Nathan over his sin, David repented sorrowfully. His most beautiful prayer of repentance can be found in Psalm 51.

Jesus does not leave us nor forsake us when we mess up or fail. He will forgive, cleanse, and restore us. However, God does not alleviate all consequences of our failure, because David's first child with Bathsheba died. Yet, God knows how to bring good even out of the failures and messes we have made. For David and Bathsheba's second son, Solomon, eventually became the wisest king ever, other than God Himself.

May we never repeat the mistakes of our past, yet may we learn from them. If we will confess and sincerely repent of all our failures, Jesus will make a miracle out of our mess.

Day 8 Let Go and Let God

…Let us lay aside every weight, and the sin which does so easily beset us, and let us run with patience the race that is set before us.

Hebrews 12:1

To live victoriously in Jesus we must be willing to confront and to let go of things that are preventing us from our best. It could be, among other things, having a disrespectful or critical attitude, terrible time management, quick temper, bad manners, or an addiction.

Jesus is constantly working on us about things in our lives in order to elevate us to new levels. We should not ignore, or even worse, justify our problem areas and simply hope that they will eventually go away. We cannot overcome them until we face them. As we humble ourselves in faith, asking Jesus for help, He will liberate us and lift us up.

If we do our part by confronting and laying aside anything that is preventing us from being our best, God will do His part by helping us win the victory over it. "Humble yourselves therefore under the mighty hand of God, that he may exalt you in due time" (I Peter 5:6).

Day 9 Overtaken by God's Blessings

And all these blessings shall come on you, and overtake you, if you shall hearken unto the voice of the Lord your God.

Deuteronomy 28:2

If we will continuously honor God by obeying His Word, opportunities will present themselves to us without us even trying to make them happen. Honoring God draws the right people, resources, and influence in our lives, and the blessings of the Lord shall OVERTAKE us.

Jesus always gives His best to those who leave their choices to Him. Blessings, favor, wisdom, and validation are drawn to us like a magnet as we honor Him with our life. Seemingly out of nowhere opportunities arise, our health improves, our debts are paid, and our dreams become reality. This is no coincidence. It is God's favor on our lives! His blessings have overtaken us!

Day 10 Open Our Eyes Lord

And Elisha prayed, and said, Lord, I pray you, open his eyes, that he may see. And the Lord opened the eyes of the young man; and he saw: and, behold, the mountain was full of horses and chariots of fire round about Elisha.

2 Kings 6:17

Before God opened the eyes of the young man assisting Elisha, he could only see fearfully that they were encircled by the Syrian army. Surprisingly, he was suddenly able to see a heavenly army of angels with horses and chariots of fire surrounding the enemy.

Often, we feel trapped and surrounded by problems and chaos, yet if Jesus were to open our spiritual eyes, we would see a mighty angelic host guarding and protecting us and warring against the dark forces of our lives. If we only center on what we can see physically, we will become afraid and disheartened. We should open our eyes of faith today so that we may see that every problem and hindrance we are facing is surrounded by the forces of our Most High God. He will fight for, protect, and advance us forward!

Jesus is greater than all the forces against us! Remember, outlook determines outcome and victory is never achieved alone.

Day 11 Safe and Secure

...So Daniel was taken up out of the den, and no manner of hurt was found upon him, because he believed in his God.

Daniel 6:23

Ungodly and jealous enemies conspired against Daniel, causing him to be arrested and thrown into the lions' den for continuing his worship of God, contrary to the arrogant king's decree. Daniel should have been torn in pieces, yet God supernaturally protected him, so much so that he incurred not even a single scratch!

Although the things we have been through may have destroyed the average person, Jesus wants each of His children to know today that He has got us! He will protect us and turn things around for our good. For those who have tried to destroy us, their evil schemes shall fall upon them.

Jesus does not typically remove us from threats, but uses them to bring us closer to Him. Our security comes in our nearness to Jesus, not in our distance from our enemies.

Day 12 The Anchor Holds

Which hope we have as an anchor of the soul, both sure and steadfast…

Hebrews 6:19

We cannot build our hopes on the basis of confusion and misery. Hope is a desire accompanied by confident expectation of or belief in fulfillment.

When we are anchored in hope, nothing can upset us, for we know Jesus is on the throne. Distracting tempests in life may try to get us to release our anchor, but if we do, we will drift away into uncertainty, pessimism and despair.

We should not place our hope in people or circumstances. Rather, let us put our hope in the Most High God, Creator of all things. Only when we are anchored in Jesus are we "sure and steadfast."

The anchor holds, though the ship is battered

The anchor holds, though the sails are torn

I have fallen on my knees, As I faced the raging seas

The anchor holds, in spite of the storm!

(Chewning & Boltz).

Day 13 Resurrection Power

Jesus said unto her [Mary], Said I not unto you, that, if you would believe, you should see the glory of God?

John 11:40

Jesus left immediately to come to Lazarus as soon as He had received word that Lazarus was sick; yet, Lazarus died four days before Jesus could get to him. Lazarus's sister Mary said to Jesus, "Lord, if You had been here, my brother would not have died." Despite the impossible circumstances, Jesus raised Lazarus from the dead!

Jesus will often have us wait on our purpose until the vision for its fulfillment is dead and buried, where the situation appears utterly impossible to ever come to pass. God's thoughts and ways are so much higher and wiser than ours. Lazarus's sisters had hoped and prayed for their brother's healing, yet Jesus planned for a resurrection.

Jesus does not usually answer our prayers the way we intended…but keep holding on! He has something greater in mind than we could possibly have imagined. He is working behind the scenes to resurrect what we thought was dead.

Day 14 New Creation

Therefore if any man be in Christ, he is a new creature: old things are passed away; behold, all things are become new.

2 Corinthians 5:17

Information in our DNA can be used to identify our biological characteristics. It can also be tested to determine emphatically who our family members are.

We became a new creation when we surrendered our lives to Jesus Christ. Suppose a test exists to sample DNA from our Heavenly Father and us. It would reveal a perfect match, without any doubt, God is our Father and we are His children! Hallelujah, we have the spiritual DNA of Jesus! Therefore, we should never think of ourselves as being ordinary. Royal blood flows through our veins. We are children of the Most High God! Our Father creates worlds!

"You are of God, little children, and have overcome them: because greater is he that is in you, than he that is in the world" (I John 4:4). We were created to excel. Our potential is limitless. Keep stretching to new levels! In Jesus name!

Day 19 Treasures of the Heart

. . . I will walk within my house with a perfect heart.

Psalm 101:2

God desires that we have perfect hearts toward Him. He sees hearts as we see faces. Jesus approves more of someone with a heart toward Him, even if this person falters, than of someone who lives righteously, yet has wrong motives.

When our hearts are perfect toward Jesus, we humbly seek His will and try to always please Him. We surrender our lives to Him and readily receive correction, so He can shape our character and so we can spiritually mature and reach new levels.

"Where your pleasure is, there is your treasure; Where your treasure is, there is your heart; Where your heart is, there is your happiness" (Augustine). We must keep all earthly treasures out of our hearts, and let Jesus be our treasure, and give Him our heart. May we love Jesus perfectly, remain close to Him, and serve Him with our whole hearts.

Day 16 Begin Again

For I know the thoughts that I think toward you, says the Lord, thoughts of peace, and not of evil, to give you an expected end.

Jeremiah 29:11

Sometimes we may think that we have fallen so far or made such terrible mistakes that we cannot be redeemed. God is more powerful than our failures and mistakes. Rather than thinking we are damaged, broken, or are filled with distrust, we should reframe it to "I'm healing, I'm rediscovering myself, I'm starting over."

If we will humble ourselves and open our hearts in returning to Jesus, He will cleanse and renew us. The toughest battle is between hanging on and letting go. Yet, nothing in the world should prevent us from letting go of the past and beginning again. Don't give up…just start over. Jesus loves us and He specializes in giving people a fresh start!

Day 17 Protected by God

O Daniel, servant of the living God, is your God, whom you serve continually, able to deliver you from the lions?

Daniel 6:20

Each of us has felt surrounded before by spiteful enemies who wanted to throw us to the lions. It is really strange how sometimes those we would take a bullet for are the ones behind the trigger ready to destroy us.

It may seem for us, like Daniel, that the more we pray the worse things become. God honored Daniel's faith by protecting him from the lions and by destroying his enemies. It may appear your friends have forsaken or even turned against you, and you are being thrown into a den of lions. Be encouraged, for Jesus has the last say in the matter! Keep trusting and believing in Him, for He has promised to never leave nor forsake us.

Jesus will close the lions' mouths, quash our accusers, and deliver us. Following all the hurtful accusations, the powerful Truth has come and declared, "YOU ARE FREE!"

Day 18 Optimism Over Pessimism

But thanks be to God, which gives us the victory through our Lord Jesus Christ.

1 Corinthians 15:57

When we experience seemingly insufferable circumstances in our lives, we can become discouraged and start to feel they will never improve. The Bible tells us that we can "triumph in Christ" (2 Corinthians 2:14).

We should never allow ourselves to become negative and bitter. Even before we fell into our problems, Jesus had the solution. He has already prepared for our victory and the next phase of our lives. Faith in God does not keep us from experiencing trials and hardships, but it enables us to endure them courageously and to emerge victoriously.

May we keep the faith and an optimistic attitude, for our God is good. He is leading us onward into the victorious life He as prepared for us!

Day 19 Our Provider

But my God shall supply all your need according to his riches in glory by Christ Jesus.

Philippians 4:19

Right now, we have all we need to realize our God-given purpose. Jesus wants us to trust in His provision for our needs. Sometimes that provision requires us to step out in faith and use what resources He has given us. He can multiply our efforts when we trust Him.

Realizing Jesus is with us, we have no cause for fear. His eye is upon us and His ear is open unto our prayers. His grace is sufficient, and His promises unmovable. May we be encouraged that we have what we need for today, and what we need for tomorrow is already prepared.

Jesus is watching over our lives closely. If we keep our focus on the Provider, rather than the provision, He will continue to provide. Jesus is our source and supply.

Day 20 Holding on to Our Destiny

The steps of a good man are ordered by the Lord: and he delights in his way.

Psalm 37:23

God has birthed a divine purpose within each of us. Someone else will control our destiny if we do not allow Jesus to order our steps.

Those who are not following their divine purpose will often try to discourage us from achieving ours, by emphasizing all the things that could go wrong, all the impossibilities associated with it, or by misdirecting our energy and focus away from God's destiny.

We should not allow family, friends, co-workers, or anyone to keep us from trusting and believing in the dreams and divine purpose that Jesus has birthed in us. May we ignore the discouraging and distracting influences and focus on God's Word and stay in alignment with Him. He believes in us, that we are ready, equipped, and capable. We are anointed and appointed by the Most High God to fulfill the destiny He has placed in us!

"The quality of our thoughts determine our actions and our actions develop our habit. Our habit creates our character and our character forges our destiny" (Stephen Covey).

Day 21 Raise the Bar

…I will make my covenant between me and you, and will multiply you exceedingly.

Genesis 17:2

Jesus wants to bring increase to our lives EXCEEDINGLY! He desires to make us greater, more influential, stronger, talented, and blessed.

As we apply ourselves to making the right decisions and staying disciplined to our purpose, God will bring the needed increase in our lives. A key quality in order to achieve is to keep improving each day and setting goals that we surpass each year. We grow our talents and skills through unswerving faith, practice and gradual learning. The Bible brings such life, health, peace, wisdom, and an abundance so that we should never be poor any longer.

"…I am come that they might have life, and that they might have it more abundantly" (John 10:10). Let us always keep raising the bar for ourselves, inspire others to do the same, and our God will multiply us exceedingly!

Day 22 Arise to Victory

I waited patiently for the Lord; and he inclined unto me, and heard my cry. He brought me up also out of an horrible pit, out of the miry clay, and set my feet upon a rock, …And he has put a new song in my mouth, even praise unto our God.

Psalm 40:1-3

At times, we have all felt as though we were in a hopeless pit of despair. In the same way that God brought David out of despair, He will lift us. Depression, sickness, heartache and pain are not the final chapter for our lives. Jesus will not leave us nor forsake us in the pit of despair.

We cannot achieve victory, if we plan for defeat. No longer will we dwell or speak negatively about problems, because praise must precede victory. God inhabits our praises.

We should bring Jesus into our situation with praise. As we exalt Him, He will lift us up out of the horrible pit and set our feet on a solid foundation. Try praising Jesus through song. Certainly if David, fighting his enemies, running from King Saul, and hiding in mountains and caves could sing praises to the Lord, we can too. Apostle Paul sang hymns that brought freedom, not only for himself, but for everyone around him. Jesus gives us a new song, a song of PRAISE and VICTORY!

Day 23 Facing Fear with Faith

Fear not; for I am with you: be not dismayed; for I am your God: I will strengthen you; yea, I will help you; yea, I will uphold you with the right hand of my righteousness.

Isaiah 41:10

Whenever we encounter circumstances in our lives that are out of our control, we can easily become disheartened, allowing fear to enter in. Fear is a self-induced prison that prevents us from experiencing freedom that God intends for us.

We should realize that God is with us, holding us up with His right hand, and that nothing is too challenging or impossible for Him to fix. We have power, victory, strength, provision and all we will ever need in the hands of Jesus Christ our Lord. If we will focus our hearts and minds on Him over our circumstances and obey His Word, we will experience supernatural breakthroughs that can advance us farther than we ever dreamed possible.

When we realize the fact that Jesus is on our side, that He is prepared to walk with us through every situation, we can easily understand why He tells us not to fear. God will not fail us. As He holds us with His powerful and caring right hand, we can face our fears with faith daily!

Day 24 Praises Go Up, Blessings Come Down

But thanks be to God, which gives us the victory through our Lord Jesus Christ.

I Corinthians 15:57

Jesus desires to give His favor to us, so we may live victoriously. This Scripture means He always gives us the victory, regardless of what we face.

If we are struggling with sickness, healing is ours. If we are heartbroken from a relationship, peace, emotional healing, and rebuilding is ours. If we have strayed from the Lord, He wants to grant forgiveness and spiritual restoration. Whatever we need, God's favor gives us provision and supplies all our needs according to His riches in glory.

If we murmur and complain about our present circumstances, we will stay in it; but, if we will praise Jesus in the midst of our struggle, He will lift us up out of it. May we open the door for His favor by offering thanksgiving, praise, and worship to our Mighty God in the eye of the storm.

Let us magnify Jesus instead of our problems! As our praises go up to Him, His blessings will come down to us.

Day 25 We Ain't Seen Nothing Yet

The glory of this latter house shall be greater than of the former, says the Lord of hosts.

Haggai 2:9

The house of God is not made of bricks and mortar, nor can it be made by human hands. We are the house of God. Jesus dwells in our hearts! "…Know you not that your body is the temple of the Holy Ghost…" (I Corinthians 6:19).

The lesson that God wants to impress upon us is that He always does a new and unique work. What is coming in our future is better for our present situation than the past. Keep on working, Jesus is with us. When He is with us we need not worry about how it will turn out. Things may be different but they will also be better.

God wants us to realize that we ain't seen nothing yet, compared to what He desires to do in our lives. The blessing and favor of our past has been wonderful, but He is going to exceed this. He is a God of increase, with much greater in store for our future!

Now is the time to expand our vision, having confident expectation that He will grant new blessings and opportunities. From this day forward, a new vision will govern our lives. From this moment on, it is going to be ALL THINGS ARE POSSIBLE. Our future glory and blessing is about to blow our minds!

Day 26 Our True Identity

And you shall know the truth, and the truth shall make you free.

John 8:32

People often try to put labels on us that are not in agreement with who Jesus says we are. If we accept them as truth, the labels can hinder us from our destiny.

These labels only have power over us that we give to them. We are not the victim of the world, but rather primarily responsible in determining our own destiny. Our choices and decisions determine whether we achieve the destiny God has for us.

We should throw off any negative labels and negative comments about us that people may have said, and embrace the truth of Jesus regarding ourselves. He labels us chosen, royal, capable, strong, precious, and victors. He determines our destiny, not people. May we resist negative things spoken over us today and accept God's Word regarding our true identity.

Day 27 Lasting Happiness

O satisfy us early with your mercy; that we may rejoice and be glad all our days.

Psalm 90:14

Joy comes from within and happiness from without. Joy depends on our relationship with Jesus, while happiness depends on our circumstances. Joy sustains, yet happiness is fleeting. Lasting happiness can only endure if we have joy within.

In order to live a happy life, we must determine that we will be happy regardless of our circumstances. We may have problems to solve and trials to endure, yet we must not allow them to steal our joy. We should start every day considering all we have to be grateful for. "This is the day which the Lord has made; we will rejoice and be glad in it" (Psalm 118:24). Being happy and grateful for what we have and where we are in life allows Jesus to bring increase to us and to get us to where He desires us to be.

Our happiness is not predicated on how much we possess, but how much we enjoy. May Jesus give us joy within that we may experience lasting happiness!

Day 28 God's Promises Fulfilled

He did not waver at the promise of God through unbelief; but was strong in faith, giving glory to God.

Romans 4:20

Abraham was unwavering regarding God's promises, in spite of his impossible circumstances. God had promised that he and his wife, Sarah, would have a child, even though they were far past childbearing years. How did Abraham handle the situation? He became "strong in faith, giving glory to God!" He was faithful and glorified the Lord, because he knew his promised son would come and that God was faithful to keep His Word. He continued praising the Lord for what was engrained in his heart and soul. God's promise to him was ultimately fulfilled.

We too should praise the Lord while we wait for His promises. We may be in an impossible situation beyond our control. Yet, Jesus has spoken promises deep in our hearts, and we know that we know that we know, that what our God has spoken, He will bring to pass. What He has started, He will finish.

May we continue to grow strong in faith as we wait on the Lord. Continue seeking Him in prayer, trusting and anticipating His fulfilled promises in our lives. Let us commit to glorifying God regardless of our difficult circumstances. Determine to walk daily with Jesus, to meditate on His Word to discover encouragement, health, and power for living. May we be strengthened in our most holy faith!

Day 29 Tried, Yet Still Trusting

That the trial of your faith, being much more precious than of gold that perishes, though it be tried with fire, might be found unto praise and honor and glory at the appearing of Jesus Christ.

I Peter 1:7

Something important for us to realize is that in this life, Jesus will not keep us from ever having problems or challenges. He knows we could never grow without experiencing them.

God wants our faith to grow stronger during fiery trials. It is easy for us to become disgruntled and negative during such times; but, in order for us to reach new levels, we must endure with positive faith and trust, bringing praise, honor, and glory to Jesus. Endurance measures our spiritual fitness. Our faith and endurance grows each time we refuse to give up.

May we stand strong in the tough times and determine to bless the Lord regardless of our circumstances and trust that Jesus is leading us in paths of righteousness for His name's sake. "Perseverance is more than endurance. It is endurance combined with absolute assurance and certainty that what we are looking for is going to happen" (Oswald Chambers).

Day 30 Love the Unlovable

Love your enemies, do good to them which hate you, Bless them that curse you, and pray for them which despitefully use you…And as you would that men should do to you, do you also to them likewise.

Luke 6:27-28 & 31

A close study of verse twenty-seven reveals that we are to love our enemies in such a way that we attempt to rescue them from their hate. Loving some individuals is very difficult, especially when they are unlovable, particularly when they do not appear to love anyone else or even desire to be loved.

Jesus provided the perfect example of this command in His life and ultimately in His death on the cross. Love releases extraordinary redemptive and life-changing power. When showing kindness in our actions and loving in our hearts to our enemies is not always easy, the Holy Spirit can fill us with the love of Jesus and enable us to live amazing grace-filled lives, even in the midst of people who hate us.

When we behave toward unlovable people the way we want to be treated, we are following the principle of the Golden Rule, "Do unto others as you would have them do unto you." Abiding by this principle releases immeasurable joy, love, and peace in our lives and pleases the Lord. Let us ask Him to help us in loving everyone, even the unlovable. To love like Jesus means loving the unlovable. To forgive like Jesus means forgiving the unforgivable.

Day 31 Love and Faith Win

There is no fear in love; but perfect love casts out fear…

I John 4:18

Fear is the major weapon the enemy uses to prevent us from progressing and enjoying the blessed life God has for us. Satan does everything in his power trying to take our focus away from our loving and faithful God. Loving Jesus is the antidote to fear and worry.

Love for Jesus inoculates us from the harmful and painful symptoms brought about by fear. The presence of love for and hope in the invincible sovereignty of God drives out fear. No matter what we are facing today, Jesus is greater than our worries, problems, and fears. He knows our every need and delights in caring for us.

"The Lord is my light and my salvation; whom shall I fear? the Lord is the strength of my life; of whom shall I be afraid?" (Psalm 27:1). When we are filled with faith, Satan is filled with fear. Let us keep our faith strong each day, so we can keep our enemy fearful of us. Fear has lost. Faith wins!

Day 32 Our Solid Rock

. . . I will never leave you, nor forsake you.

Hebrews 13:5

Although we may be facing challenging times and are dealing with things we do not fully understand, we should trust Jesus and remember that He is always with us through it all. He never said that we would not have difficulties, but He did say that He would never leave us nor forsake us. He is working all things together to benefit us (see Romans 8:28).

Jesus protects us from becoming too worldly, draws us closer to Him, teaches us patience, increases our faith, and so much more. During tough times let us take hold of the Rock which cannot be moved, Jesus Christ. "The Lord is my rock, and my fortress, and my deliverer; my God, my strength, in whom I will trust; my buckler, and the horn of my salvation, and my high tower" (Psalm 18:2).

When we trust Jesus through everything that is happening, He secures us and fills us with more of Him—more of His love, more of His joy, and more of His peace. "I have set the Lord always before me: because he is at my right hand, I shall not be moved" (Psalm 16:8).

Day 33 Everything's Going to be Alright

Now faith is the substance of things hoped for, the evidence of things not seen.

Hebrews 11:1

According to this Scripture, faith is the evidence of things not seen. There are promises in the Bible that we cannot always see with our physical eyes. Even though we cannot see them, we must decide to believe that these promises are true.

It is easy to fall into negativity when others are fearful all around us and circumstances appear bleak at best. Fear is the polar opposite of faith. Faith does not look at what is happening to us, instead it focuses on Jesus in whom we trust. Faith makes life bearable, with all its crises and uncertainties, yet the only way we can develop strong faith is by enduring great trials. Our job is to keep trusting Jesus while He works on our behalf.

We should keep moving forward! Our toughest times usually lead to the greatest moments of our lives. Difficult situations develop strong people in the end. Remember, there is never a moment when God is not in control. So just relax! Jesus has us covered. The last page of the Bible lets us know that everything's going to be alright.

Day 34 Faith's Reward

If we hope for that we see not, then do we with patience wait for it.

Romans 8:25

We may not be good at waiting. But, our hope in the Lord gives us patience that is beyond our human inclination. As much as the Lord has blessed us, we should be fully confident that the good things Jesus has in store for us is beyond our imaginations.

In the midst of any circumstance Jesus wants us to stay positive, hopeful, and guided by our faith in Him and His Word. Faith allows us to believe things that may not even seem rational to our carnal minds. Walking by faith does not mean we overlook our condition. Instead, it means we decide to center our attention on Jesus, trusting that He is superior to everything we are going through, and that He will "do exceeding abundantly above all that we ask or think, according to the power that works in us" (Ephesians 3:20).

In these uncertain times, may we trust God's Word over our fear and doubt, and proclaim words of faith to our circumstances. Faith allows us to believe the unbelievable. Hope causes us to hope when all seems hopeless. Faith's reward is seeing what we believe. Therefore, while we patiently wait, we should try to stay busy…busy loving God and sharing His mercy and grace with others.

Day 35 Winners Never Quit

Therefore endure hardness, as a good soldier of Jesus Christ.

2 Timothy 2:3

Notice that the Apostle Paul never warns believers away from their trials. Paul obviously felt that his life was richer from following Christ in such a way and he desired for others to experience that richness too.

Becoming upset or discouraged concerning hard times never changes them. However, choosing to apply positivity in our minds, the things we say, and with our attitude makes a HUGE difference in how we are able to cope and eventually become victorious.

God's Word promises that if we rely on Him, we will not be tested more than we are able to bear and that He will make a way of escape or endurance for us (see 1 Corinthians 10:13). Jesus uses difficult times to show Himself strong in and through us, guiding us to new levels and opportunities (see 2 Corinthians 12:9). Strengthening our faith requires enduring severe trials and testing; and, our endurance grows each time we resist giving up. "Losers quit when they fail. Winners fail until they succeed" (Robert Kiyosaki). The moment when we are hardest pressed to quit is the time Jesus is about to work a miracle!

Our richness may not come in prison like Paul's experience, but we can be sure we do experience the richness that God has in store for us. This may bring hardship and often suffering, yet it will also bring blessings beyond belief.

Day 36 Peace Within

Be careful for nothing; but in everything by prayer and supplication with thanksgiving let your requests be made known unto God. And the peace of God, which passes all understanding, shall keep your hearts and minds through Christ Jesus.

Philippians 4:6-7

God desires to hear and receive our prayers. However, to prevent them from being too self-centered, God asks us to always give thanks.

We can easily turn prayer into a wish list. The absence of praise and thanksgiving with our prayers leaves them lacking or empty. Leaving off praise causes our hearts to darken, because all we consider is our problems and prayer becomes a request line.

When we release all our worries and fears to Jesus in prayer and praise, we gain a new perspective in which He becomes magnified in our eyes and our problems become smaller and less significant. He replaces our fears by giving hope, peace, joy, and love. Regardless of all our troubles, may we remain focused on Jesus and accept His wonderful and glorious peace and security. Genuine peace must come from within.

"We cannot change or control the world around us, but we can change and control the world within ourselves" (Warren Wiersbe). Only when we have peace within ourselves can we bring peace to others.

Day 37 The Greatest Exercise for the Heart

Give, and it shall be given unto you; good measure, pressed down, and shaken together, and running over, shall men give into your bosom…

Luke 6:38

Our blessings are based on our willingness to bless others. Our test of treating and judging others will be the basis used for how we are treated and judged by others and by Jesus.

True contentment comes when we discover the joy of taking our focus off ourselves, realizing we have a higher purpose, primarily to dedicate our lives to making a positive impact on others and our world. In Mark 10:30, Jesus tells us that anything we sacrifice for the gospel's sake, He will restore it unto us a hundredfold in this life!

We cannot be like Jesus without being generous givers with our time, talent, and resources. Being generous causes us to be astonished at how happy we have become and how much more we enjoy life. The greatest exercise for our hearts is to lift others up. The greatest reward comes from doing something for someone who cannot repay us. In giving we receive. We may give without loving, but it is impossible to love without giving.

Day 38 Jesus First

And you shall seek me, and find me, when you shall search for me with all your heart.

Jeremiah 29:13

Spending time with Jesus should be the number one priority in our schedules. Our quality of life is directly correlated with the quality of time we spend with Him.

Our time with God can easily become interrupted or replaced by "more urgent" matters because we assume He will always be there. However, if we continue to ignore Him, eventually Jesus becomes an afterthought in our day, only receiving the leftovers of our lives. Eventually, we slowly lose our connectedness to Him. Jesus must be our first priority!

If we just focus on Jesus and keeping Him first, then everything else will fall into place more easily. Putting Him first enables us to live victoriously and fills our lives with His joy, peace and love. We should make sure our activities and our attitudes align with what pleases the Lord first and foremost. What we focus our attention on the most will become the guiding force in our lives.

May Jesus bless us with undivided hearts, ones that seek Him as the first priority of our lives. Ask Him to forgive us for allowing other things to distract our attention from Him and that have interfered with our devotion to His kingdom. May God infill us with a sacred passion for His will above all other responsibilities and interests.

Day 39 Our Great Reward

Cast not away therefore your confidence, which has great recompense of reward.

Hebrews 10:35

We experience some tough times in life. They are inescapable. During such times is when our confidence in God and His Word are tested. If we will continue to walk in faith, believing and trusting in Jesus, all the promises of His Word are available to us. He promises great reward! Sometimes the promise takes longer than anticipated. People frequently miss out on God's best by quitting just before their answer comes.

Our faith cannot take a break when we struggle through the belly of hell. So do not throw it away. Press on! May we keep putting one foot before the other, trusting that Jesus will give us the strength for another step. Regardless of how hard things are at this time, refuse to give in to despair. Do not give up! Whatever we have been waiting for, keep holding on. Our promise is closer than we realize. Even if our situation seems worse than ever, let this be a sign that we are nearer to victory. Our God is faithful and He will not fail!

Let us not cast off our confidence, for our great reward is almost here! We have come too far for far too long to quit now! May we determine to patiently and confidently wait for the promise of our great reward, and allow the promises of God to shine on all our problems today.

Day 40 Victory in Jesus

But thanks be to God, which gives us the victory through our Lord Jesus Christ.

1 Corinthians 15:57

Jesus conquered sin and death so we could live righteously, abundantly, and victoriously. The anointing, which is the resurrection power of Jesus that we have received, abides in us today. We activate this resurrection power by believing it, speaking it, and acting on it.

The resurrection power of God is the most powerful force in the universe! Regardless of any type of sin or stronghold that tries to imprison us as Spirit-filled believers, we have power and authority over it in Jesus name! His anointing destroys every yoke of bondage! Jesus defeated Satan through His death and resurrection. Because of His victory, Jesus has empowered us to overcome every temptation and has given sufficient resources for us to respond biblically to any difficulty in life. By depending on the power of His Spirit and remaining obedient to His Word, we can conquer any obstacle.

We should never accept defeat in our lives, for Jesus paid too great a price for us to accept anything less than total and complete VICTORY. Life is ours! Death no longer holds us captive! Victory is ours! Jesus is Lord!

Day 41 Rejoice and Be Glad

This is the day which the Lord has made; we will rejoice and be glad in it.

Psalm 118:24

Each day, we should arise with an attitude of gratitude, filled with confident expectation of what Jesus has planned. Everything may not be perfect in our lives and we may have difficulties to deal with. Yet, may we determine to magnify the Lord instead of magnifying our problems.

We will be glad in that Jesus is with us and will never forsake us, that He will supply all our needs according to His riches in glory, and that He has prepared a place for us to live with Him eternally in Heaven. This is a great day to be alive!

We will rejoice and be exceedingly glad. King Jesus still reigns and everything is going to be alright, for He is fighting our battles. Our God will never fail us! We will always win if we put our faith in Him daily, keep standing, and refuse to quit.

Day 42 A Good Name

A good name is rather to be chosen than great riches, and loving favor rather than silver and gold.

Proverbs 22:1

Consider what others think whenever they hear your name. Do they think you are trustworthy, a person who keeps your word and can be depended on to do what is right and decent? Or, do they think everyone should be cautious of you and that you cannot be trusted? Then compare that to how you think of yourself. "Every way of a man is right in his own eyes…" (Proverbs 21:2).

Jesus desires for us to be people of integrity, respect, and truthfulness. People with integrity do whatever is right even when nobody is watching them. As children of the Most High God, we should be the same in private as we are in public. We do not need a signed contract to pressure us into keeping our promises.

When all is said and done with our lives and careers, people are going to remember our character, the way we treated them, and our loyalty to our family and to our God. Jesus will honor us with His loving favor each day if we will maintain our integrity from the smallest of matters to the most important ones. A simple way to do this is if something is not right, then don't do it; and, if something is not true, then don't say it. A treasure far greater than money and riches is being a person of integrity and excellence.

Day 43 Our Covenant of Peace

And I will make with them a covenant of peace…

Ezekiel 34:25

Regardless of what problems life may have dealt us, Jesus is with us and He will not fail! We should never feel afraid or worried, since the Most High God has made with us a "covenant of peace."

God's peace is constantly available, no matter what we may be facing. "And the peace of God, which passes all understanding, shall keep your hearts and minds through Christ Jesus" (Philippians 4:7). This means that we can have peace even during times when it may seem irrational or illogical for one to have peace! While the entire world may be fearful and troubled, we have peace within. For we have the calm assurance, if Jesus is with us, then all the life, strength, provision, love, peace, and joy we will ever need is present. He shall supply all our needs when the economy fails. He heals all our diseases during epidemics or pandemics. He is our refuge and mighty fortress against all evil and violence in the world.

Jesus will prepare the way before us and will keep us in perfect peace as our minds are stayed upon Him (see Isaiah 26:3). This is the prerequisite to the covenant of peace. Our minds need to be focused on God and His will, rather than the trouble surrounding us in order to receive the peace part of the covenant. Let us begin by praising God for His peace, then dwell on His scriptural promises, and choose to keep our hearts and minds continually set on Him.

Day 44 Name Above All Names

Wherefore God also has highly exalted him, and given him a name which is above every name: That at the name of Jesus every knee should bow, of things in heaven, and things in earth, and things under the earth.

Philippians 2:9

The name of Jesus is above every name in Heaven and on Earth. His name is greater than earthly kings, presidents, or individuals of great wealth and prestige. His name is far above and more powerful than Kennedy, Rockefeller, Bezos, Trump, Gates, Zuckerberg, and Buffet.

The name of Jesus supersedes any other known name. His name has power over all sin, sickness, poverty, and authority. Only the name of Jesus provides salvation, healing, power, love, joy, peace, deliverance, provision, and blessings. The list of all that is available to us through His name is limitless.

God says, "…I have even called you by your name: I have surnamed you…" (Isaiah 45:4). By taking on His name, we have been granted God's power and authority, having access to His storehouse of blessings. Everything He has is available to us in Jesus name. "If you shall ask anything in my name, I will do it" (John 14:14).

Day 45 Love and Honor Others

But Jesus, said unto them, A prophet is not without honor, but in his own country, and among his own kin, and in his own house. And he could do no mighty work there … And he marveled because of their unbelief…

Mark 6:4–6

The people of the area where Jesus grew up, family and friends, did not honor Him nor believe that He was the Messiah. This adversely impacted their ability to receive His blessing.

One way we honor the Lord is to honor the people He has placed in our lives. How we regard them affects our relationship with God. "Inasmuch as ye have done it unto one of the least of these my brethren, ye have done it unto me" (Matthew 25:40).

Today, we should determine to honor those which God has placed in our lives, so Jesus can work mightier in our own life. Focus on the value and the good in others, whether it be family, friends, or co-workers. As we show respect and honor toward them, our faith will grow stronger and we will develop godly character and position ourselves to receive all the blessings the Lord has stored up for us. May Jesus show us how to love and honor people in our lives the way He loves us.

Day 46 Perfect Strength

He gives power to the faint; and to them that have no might he increases strength.

Isaiah 40:29

Even the most motivated and positive individuals among us find ourselves broken-down and weary at some point in our lives. It is easy to believe and follow Jesus when we are soaring on eagles' wings. In times of utter powerlessness, weakness, and brokenness Jesus usually is most real, powerful, and present to us.

We have all felt weary and overwhelmed by the circumstances of life. Waiting for God's strength and deliverance is usually accompanied by fear, stress, and even grief. Jesus has promised power and protection for those who wait for Him. If we will put our faith in His Word and trust in His love and wisdom, Jesus will strengthen us to endure the struggles. Additionally, He will also help us spiritually mature through the process. Regardless of what we are facing, our God is greater than any obstacle we face. We should not attempt to make it on our own strength, but cast ourselves at the feet of Jesus.

When we have no strength, we can lean on Jesus for the strength we need. "His strength is perfect when our strength is gone. He'll carry us when we can't carry on. Raised in His power the weak become strong. His strength is perfect" (Jerry Salley & Steven Curtis Chapman). May we persist in prayer today and let faith flood our hearts so we can be strong in the Lord and in the power of His might!

Day 47 Making Something Out of Nothing

And the earth was without form, and void; and darkness was upon the face of the deep. And the Spirit of God moved upon the face of the waters. And God said, Let there be light: and there was light.

Genesis 1:2-3

Today's passage informs us that God created the universe out of nothing. If our God can make something out of nothing, then He can surely speak to the seemingly impossible situations in our lives and create something glorious and wonderful as well! Jesus can speak light to our darkness, give us hope in the midst of our despair, and transform us into powerful and strong individuals by His Spirit.

We are most powerful and capable when our life aligns with His Word. Nothing, no individual, no army, no stronghold can stand against our God! Only Jesus can give us freedom in our struggles. His power is not limited by our circumstances.

Faith can open doors and create opportunities for accessing God's power against all odds. Let us trust Jesus to make a way where there seems to be no way, overflow our hearts and minds with His peace and joy, and open our spiritual eyes to walk by faith.

Day 48 Until Our Change Comes

...All the days of my appointed time will I wait, till my change come.

Job 14:14

Jesus desires to raise us to higher levels and for us to develop and enlarge each area of our lives. Change is necessary for this to happen. Zig Ziglar says, "Little men with little minds and little imaginations go through life in little ruts, smugly resisting all changes which would jar their little worlds." It is always after we have moved beyond our comfort zone that we begin to change and grow.

As we submit to the process of allowing Scripture to govern our lives and for the Holy Spirit to guide us, Jesus will open and close doors so we remain on the correct path to our divine purpose. At just the right time and because Jesus loves us immeasurably, He will pry us from our comfort level in order to stretch us. He cares far too deeply to allow us to live a life of mediocrity.

There are no accidents in the life of a devout Christian...everything happens for a purpose. We must be open to change in order to grow. During our challenging times we occasionally think we will surely fall. Yet, these difficulties become the very force of change that drive us to the destiny God has awaiting us. Today, let us trust Jesus and His ability to change things in our lives for the better.

Day 49 Never Changing God…Change Us

Jesus Christ the same yesterday, and today, and forever.

Hebrews 13:8

For I am the Lord, I change not…" (Malachi 3:6). Our God is not progressive, constantly changing, or evolving. He is already holy, righteous, and perfect. However, we should evolve daily into becoming more like Him—in love, forgiveness, holiness, and patience.

The problem with pseudo-Christians is that they keep trying to change God and mold Him into the God they want Him to be for them. In doing so, they lead others down their dangerous path away from the Lord's will. The Bible is inspired of God and the final authority for our lives. May God help us to allow Scripture to speak to us and the Holy Spirit to guide us down the path of daily molding into the image of Christ Jesus.

The concern is not whether we are challenged. Rather, the question is have we been changed? Are we willing to change? Will we allow God to change us from the inside out? We always face the agony of choice before the promise of change. "We can create as magnificent an environment as we like, but unless we change the heart it's all a waste of time" (John Hagee). Let us pray for Jesus to change us as He sees fit!

Day 50 More than Enough

And God is able to make all grace abound toward you; that you, always having all sufficiency in all things, may abound to every good work.

2 Corinthians 9:8

Jesus is more than enough for whatever we need. He is a God of abundance. The term abound used in this verse means "cause to super-abound or excel." When our appropriately-placed beliefs and expectations align with His Word, Jesus is more than able to provide healing, move obstacles, resurrect hopes that we may have given up on, and give us the strength and courage to face any difficulties that may come our way.

As we walk humbly and according to His Word, our Lord extends His loving favor over our lives and opens the windows of Heaven to bless us abundantly above our expectations. We have all that we need and more! When we are blessed with more than enough, we are even in a position to bless others around us.

Jesus desires to overtake us with His loving favor and fullness of blessings. May He use these to draw us closer to Him daily, for Jesus is more than enough!

Day 51 The Apple of His Eye

Keep me as the apple of the eye, hide me under the shadow of thy wings.

Psalm 17:8

Being the "apple of God's eye" involves being the very center of His attention and the gateway to His heart. Believers who are kept as the apple of His eye, Jesus watches over intensely to guard and to protect. We are His delight, His exceeding joy, His prized possession, and the apple of the eye!

The wonderful reality behind this image is that, figuratively speaking, when we look into God's eyes, we see our own reflection. Why? Because our Heavenly Father's central focus is always on His children. He loves us so much! There is nothing more important or of greater value to our Lord than His children. We matter! We do not inconvenience Him by asking for His help and strength.

Jesus wants us to seek Him. He desires to bless us with His Goodness! He has a divine plan for our lives. We can cast all our care upon Him, because He truly cares for us more than anyone could ever care. Let us praise Jesus today for keeping us as the apple of His eye.

Day 52 Keep Asking

Ask, and it shall be given you; seek, and you shall find; knock, and it shall be opened unto you.

Matthew 7:7

Prayer essentially is asking God to do for us what He has promised He will do if we ask Him. What do we want or need Jesus to do for us, our family, in our finances, for our bodies? We can ask Him to bring healing, cleansing, deliverance, salvation, and anything we may need.

Ask…look…knock. Jesus expects us to be persistent, to keep asking, to continue looking, and to not give up! Today's verse is not a formula, but rather the attitude we should have with our prayers and lives. We should be persistent in prayer and faithfulness to God. Yet, before we focus heavily on being persistent, we must first seek His Kingdom and desire His will. This is confirmed in the Lord's Prayer found in Matthew 6:9-13.

God longs to give us the desires of our hearts and to shower His blessings upon us. If we will allow Jesus to be first and Lord of our lives, we will not only receive from Him, but we will be changed during the process! Instead of wishing for things to change, let us ask God for His strength to make a change today.

Day 53 Brightly Shining

But the path of the just is as the shining light, that shines more and more unto the perfect day.

Proverbs 4:18

Trying to shine on our own can be exhausting. Rather than doing this ourselves, we are to stay near to Jesus and to remain in Him. He promises that our path will shine brighter each day as we seek to live justly.

Living justly means that we seek righteousness and truth and our life stays aligned with God's Word. Aligning with His Word is about surrendering our lives to Him, obeying His commandments, and following His purpose each day. If we do this, Jesus will lead us properly in every decision we must make. His light shines forth through us in powerful, marvelous ways that help change our world and those around us.

Anytime the darkness starts creeping in, may Jesus shine in our hearts so brightly that love, joy, and peace overflows from us to others. The central goal of Christians is to be what God is. He is Light and in Him is no darkness.

Day 54 Timing is Everything

Wait on the Lord, and keep his way, and he shall exalt you to inherit the land…

Psalm 37:34

Whenever we move outside our comfort zone we start changing, growing, and spiritually maturing. Correct timing to make changes is vital to our success.

If we do not comprehend God's timing, we can become spiritually unstable, attempting to make good things happen, yet at the incorrect time. For instance, people may quit their steady job because they realize God wants them to work in a different profession or to start a new business. The job search becomes unsuccessful or the business fails from lack of funds or insurmountable debt. Feeling discouraged and frustrated, they try to survive on unemployment or charity from others. Making major changes prematurely can risk the very potential in fulfilling our God-given purpose.

Stress causes us to believe everything must happen right now. Faith assures us that it will happen in God's timing. Jesus always has an appointed time for things to happen. When we put Him first, trust in His timing, and maintain our faith…dreams come true!

Day 55 Forgetting the Past

...This one thing I do, forgetting those things which are behind, and reaching forth unto those things which are before.

Philippians 3:13

It seems impossible to completely forget our past. "Forgetting" in this verse can mean "to forget," yet also means "to neglect" or "to ignore." We deliberately ignore our past so it has minimal influence over our present lives. We do this also in order to work effectively in the present and to press toward the future.

Let us not become entangled in what has happened to us. Instead, we should move on, not only from our past failures, but from our past victories as well. Disregarding the old allows us to experience new accomplishments. If we are to soar like eagles, we need to leave the ground. If we want to move forward in life, we need to let go of the past that drags us down.

Today, we should leave the past in the past for good. Let us not permit our past to render us powerless, give it to Jesus, and praise Him for what we have learned from it. Let go of it in faith and focus our efforts on our present and what lies ahead. We press forward toward the prize Jesus has prepared for us.

Day 56 Friend of God

And the scripture was fulfilled which says, Abraham believed God, and it was imputed unto him for righteousness: and he was called the Friend of God.

James 2:23

Jesus, the Almighty God, Creator of all things desires to be our friend! To be a friend of God means we have access to the very heart of God. Friendship involves loving and being loved. Jesus is a friend who "sticks closer than a brother," which means He will always be there to support, encourage, and to strengthen us. Others may fail and disappoint, yet Jesus will never leave nor forsake us. He will be faithful to the end. He is on our side, always working things together for our good.

Jesus loves us greatly and desires our friendship. To be called the friend of God is, without a doubt, one of the greatest honors ever! Anytime we start feeling alone or think that no one cares, let us remind ourselves…"I am a friend of God!"

Day 57 Our God Wants To Do Great Things

Fear not, O land; be glad and rejoice: for the Lord will do great things.

Joel 2:21

Our Lord desires to do marvelous things in our lives. Today's Scripture begins with "fear not." With all that is currently happening in the world, fear seems to have become the norm for most people.

We may have many reasons to fear, yet fear is not of God. Fear in our hearts is the greatest hindrance to allowing God to do great things for us. Permitting fear cripples our faith. Jesus says, "…be not faithless, but believing" (John 2:27). "…For whatsoever is not of faith is sin" (Romans 14:23). We should never allow fear to influence any of our decisions. We can conquer fear by loving Jesus with all our hearts and by meditating on Scripture and praying daily.

"There is no fear in love; but perfect love casts out fear…" (I John 4:18). The deeper we fall in love with Jesus, the more we realize we have nothing to fear! Let us determine to rejoice in the Lord and trust that He will do great things in our lives. Never forget, if God is for us, no one can be against us. We are more than conquerors and overcomers in Jesus name!

Day 58 At the Feet of Jesus

But one thing is needful: and Mary has chosen that good part, which shall not be taken away from her.

Luke 10:42

Mary remained captivated at the feet of Jesus as He taught, while Martha constantly stayed busy about the house, preparing meals and such. Martha eventually complained to Jesus about Mary's lack of help with the housework. Martha seemed to think that Mary was wasting time, when there was important housework to be done. Jesus replied, "Martha, you are troubled and stressed about so many things, yet Mary has chosen the best thing to do right now."

We can become so caught up in our work and responsibilities that we neglect time in the presence of Jesus. If we are too busy to read the Bible and pray daily and enjoy weekly worship with the people of God, we have become far too busy.

Today, let us reevaluate our schedules and put Jesus first by scheduling other responsibilities around spending our time with Him. We should not try to fit Him into our schedule, but rather fit everything else into our schedule with God. The results will have eternal consequences.

Day 59 Rest for the Soul

Take my yoke upon you, and learn of me; for I am meek and lowly in heart: and you shall find rest unto your souls.

Matthew 11:29

We can easily feel overwhelmed by all the turmoil happening in the world. We may also worry about family, friends, or co-workers. Often we search for peace and rest in food, watching TV, relationships, shopping, or various other ways. These actions are not in themselves bad, yet they can never bring real peace and rest to our souls.

Casting our cares on Jesus is the only true way to find what we need. He wants us to live restful and peaceful lives. If we will spend time in His presence, we will experience peace beyond human understanding. Our rest lies in turning to the Lord, not to ourselves or other things.

Only Jesus can satisfy our souls…Only He can give us peace and make us whole…Only He can bring true joy and happiness…Only Jesus can give real meaning to our lives. He is the only answer to every question, concern, fear, and need we will ever have. May we run into the loving arms of Jesus and find the rest our hearts and souls truly long for.

Day 60 Prince of Peace

…His name shall be called …Prince of Peace

Isaiah 9:6

The Hebrew word "Shalom" is used in the Old Testament for "peace." It means more than freedom from conflict. Shalom involves people flourishing in right relationship with God, with one another, and with everything in life. Jesus is our Prince of Peace!

When it seems impossible to be at peace, Jesus gives us peace that surpasses all understanding. He can calm any storm and overcome any obstacle. The storms of life do not govern or define our lives. If we will praise Him in the midst of the storm, He will lead us to victory. He brings peace that the world could never give.

The only peace that can truly calm the soul and empower us to cope with the turmoil in our world is the peace that Jesus, the Prince of Peace, provides. To have peace in our world, we must first have peace in our own hearts and souls. Only in Jesus can we truly know peace. Only in Him can we truly say, "It is well with my soul."

Day 61 Chosen and Ordained

Before I formed you in the belly I knew you; and before you came forth out of the womb I sanctified you, and I ordained you a prophet unto the nations.

Jeremiah 1:5

God preordained Jeremiah to be a prophet, while he was in his mother's womb. Even with this great calling on his life, the path was not easy for him. He faced terrible persecution at times, so much so that he nearly gave up completely.

We may not enjoy our current surroundings, yet this is where Jesus has us at this time of our lives. We should accept where He has positioned us and allow His light to shine through in the best possible way. Jesus approves of us, and that is all that really matters. His loving favor protects us like a shield.

May we be strong and of good courage in our hearts and minds, realizing that God has chosen, called, anointed, and approved us. Jeremiah was mocked, criticized, and abused, but he declared precisely what God had sent him to prophesy. He spoke complete truth in the face of persecution and anguish. Having the approval of Jesus is of much greater importance and value than the praise of people.

"In darkness God's truth shines most clear" (Corrie Ten Boom). God's joy and peace runs deeper than despair. His will is our hiding place. May Jesus keep us in the center of His will!

Day 62 Safeguarding The Heart

Keep your heart with all diligence; for out of it are the issues of life.

Proverbs 4:23

We are to discipline ourselves considering what we allow into our hearts and minds and how we live regarding what is stored in our hearts, our internal values. Our eyes, ears, and mouths are entryways into our hearts. Anything we view, listen to, or speak opens these entrances to influencing our hearts. Remember the little children's song lyrics, "Be careful little eyes what you see…Be careful little ears what you hear…Be careful little mouth what you speak." We can safeguard our hearts by being extremely cautious about what we watch and listen to—TV, gaming, Internet, or gossip and other forms of unholy conversation. Any of these things can influence our heart drawing us into darkness.

One easy way for us to realize what is influencing us is to pay attention to what we speak. Jesus said, "Out of the abundance of the heart the mouth speaks." Our words can reveal the condition of our heart. What are we storing in our heart? Jesus sees hearts as we sees faces. Let us take inventory regarding what we see, hear, and speak and determine to safeguard our hearts by asking Jesus to guide our decisions and actions daily.

Day 63 The Gift of Joy

Restore unto me the joy of your salvation; and uphold me with your free spirit.

Psalm 51:12

Conditions of life may have stolen the joy of our salvation, yet there is great news…Jesus is in the restoration business and He wants to restore our joy today!

Jesus does not intend for us to live a life of dreariness, depression, and despair. Joy is a gift from the Lord, which we obtain by being in His presence. Joy is based entirely on our relationship with Him. The joy Jesus gives enables us to endure life's struggles and to experience freedom and rejoicing independent of our surroundings. Our hearts can be filled with delight, though the world seems to be collapsing around us.

Joy is reliant on our relationship with Jesus, rather than our circumstances. Hindrances to having joy are seeking happiness over joy, lack of time in reading and meditating on Scripture, disobedience to God and His Word, and prayerlessness. Jesus made it distinctly clear on how to regain our joy, "…Continue in my love. If you keep my commandments, you shall abide in my love; even as I have kept my Father's commandments, and abide in his love. These things have I spoken unto you, that my joy might remain in you, and that your joy might be full" (John 15:9-11).

Anytime we feel our joy drifting away it is time to enter into the presence of Jesus and declare that the joy of the Lord is our strength. Let us praise Him for the wonderful gift of joy He has given us!

Day 64 Faith Conquers Worry

Be careful for nothing; but in everything by prayer and supplication with thanksgiving let your requests be made known unto God.

Philippians 4:6

The first part of this verse emphasizes for us not to worry about anything. Worry carries tomorrow's burdens with today's strength. Worry is extremely counterproductive, robbing us of peace and joy in our lives. Worry disrupts our sleep and can even make us physically sick. However, Jesus has promised us victory over worry!

If we will choose to walk by faith, not by fear and worry, Jesus will give us peace and restore our joy. We should determine not to become constantly worry-focused on negative news. We need to stay informed; however, we should be most informed in scriptural truth, God's unfailing Word.

Feeding faith will drive out worry and will fill our hearts with confident expectation, peace, and joy. May Jesus help us to completely trust in Him every day as we declare His Word over our lives.

Day 65 Don't Hang with Turkeys

He that walks with wise men shall be wise: but a companion of fools shall be destroyed.

Proverbs 13:20

Who we spend our time with is more important than the way we spend our time. Numerous people have missed moving to new levels and achieving their destiny due to wrong friendships. A familiar saying states, "You cannot soar like an eagle if you hang with turkeys." We should not allow ourselves to hang with negative people, "turkeys," who have no dreams, aspirations, or goals. If we do, we will catch their negativity and mediocrity will infect us.

Another adage says, "A man is known by the company he keeps." We could rephrase this statement to "We become the company we keep." If we spend our time with negative, envious, miserable individuals, we will become like them. Instead, we should gravitate to or "hang" with positive and motivated people determined to succeed, who have a winning mentality, people of integrity who strive for excellence. Those positive individuals we keep company with will influence us to be better, while we do the same for them.

The company we keep reflects who we are and who we want to be. May we determine to make close friendships with individuals who uplift us and who challenge us to be our best.

Day 66 Love God's Praise Over People's

...lest they should be put out of the synagogue. For they loved the praise of men more than the praise of God.

John 12:42-43

Today's Scripture reveals that many prominent Jews believed Jesus, but would not confess their belief for they feared being ostracized by others. It is better to have God's approval than the thoughtless approval of the masses.

We lose our joy when we expect from people and things what only God can give. When we follow Jesus rather than people, we will have an inner peace and joy and realize the unique purpose He has for us. Far too many preachers today seek the approval of their congregants, so they soften their sermons. Christian leaders seek the approval of prominent public heads, so they compromise their standards. God's people often desire the approval of the world, so they become like the world; consequently, rather than changing the world, they allow the world to change them.

"Our greatest fear should not be of failure but of succeeding at things in life that don't really matter" (Francis Chan). We exalt and glorify Jesus best when we are most content in Him. Let us reverence and love Jesus Christ above all others so our joy may be full, complete, and overflowing.

Day 67 Having the Mind of Christ

For who has known the mind of the Lord, that he may instruct him? but we have the mind of Christ.

I Corinthians 2:16

The world sends a constant barrage of messages to us, attempting to distract us from what matters most by filling our minds with politics, the world, business, sex, sports, products, and numerous other things. Having the mind of Christ means we think the way Jesus thinks.

Rather than thinking negatively, fearfully, or judgmentally, we think positive, good, decent, and loving thoughts. We can defeat the devil by thinking God's thoughts and by speaking and acting on them. We should cleanse our minds from any anger, remembrance of evil, and shameful thoughts. Before we can walk as Jesus walked, and talk as He talked, we must first begin to think as He thinks.

"Let this mind be in you, which was also in Christ Jesus." (Philippians 2:5). If we have the mind of Christ, anxiety will be replaced by trust, hatred by love, and fear by faith. May we challenge ourselves to bring every thought under subjection to the Word. We will discover that we have begun to move from bondage into the mind of Christ Jesus and a life of freedom.

Day 68 Our Source of Courage

Be strong and of a good courage, fear not, nor be afraid of them: for the Lord your God, he it is that does go with you; he will not fail you, nor forsake you.

Deuteronomy 31:6

We should not live our lives controlled by fear. Do not simply wait and hope for fear to leave. Determine from this moment forward to live confidently, assertively, and positively.

Being courageous is taking action while experiencing fear within and from others around us. We increase in might, courage, and confidence with each experience requiring us to confront our fear. Overcoming what scares us the worst strengthens us the most. Action is required to overcome fear! A fearless warrior never existed. Victorious warriors fight through fear to do what must be done! Besides, we possess the ultimate source of courage…Christ within (see Ephesians 3:17).

The time has come in our lives when we must decide what is first in our lives and who is first in our lives. Are we going to be courageous or a coward? May Jesus help us to be bold and courageous. When opportunities come our way to show courage, may we resolve to stand strong and uncontrolled by fear.

Day 69 Be an Overcomer Rather than a Critic

There is therefore now no condemnation to them which are in Christ Jesus, who walk not after the flesh, but after the Spirit.

Romans 8:1

Frequently people criticize us when we are truly following the Lord. The only way we can avoid criticism is to say nothing, to do nothing, and to be nothing. Since Jesus intends to make us like Him, He will take us through experiences that are similar to those things which He experienced in order to shape us into His image.

We may have to endure periods of isolation, temptation, stress, criticism, rejection, and numerous other problems. "The way we respond to criticism pretty much depends on the way we respond to praise. If praise humbles us, then criticism will build us up. But if praise inflates us, then criticism will crush us; and both responses lead to our defeat" (Warren Wiersbe). Anyone can easily criticize, complain, and condemn, but it requires true character and self-control to be patient and forgiving.

Whenever someone criticizes us, we should think and speak positive things about ourselves. Refuse to internalize anything that people throw at us. May we remind ourselves of the love of Jesus, trust in His approval, and not allow criticism to cripple us.

Day 70 The Goodness of the Lord

I had fainted, unless I had believed to see the goodness of the Lord in the land of the living.

Psalm 27:13

People who progress best are those with positive attitudes, who are purposefully grateful, and who focus on the good that life has and can provide them. The difference between obstacles and opportunities is our attitude toward them.

Each opportunity has a problem and each problem has an opportunity. Believing negative thoughts is the single greatest barrier to success. As we nurture and promote gratitude and a positive attitude, we will experience higher levels of success and achievement.

So get ready, SOMETHING GOOD IS ABOUT TO HAPPEN! "Fear not, little flock; for it is your Father's good pleasure to give you the kingdom" (Luke 12:32).

Day 71 Authentic Christians

You have not chosen me, but I have chosen you, and ordained you, that you should go and bring forth fruit, and that your fruit should remain…

John 15:16

Saying we are Christians is simply empty words; but, living the Christian life before the world speaks volumes to everyone around us. Jesus has empowered us with His Spirit to bear fruits of genuine love, joy, peace, patience, kindness, goodness, faithfulness, gentleness and self-control with our words and actions. We personify Jesus well when these good fruits are produced in our lives.

Authenticity is one of our most important commodities. It requires vulnerability, transparency, and integrity. Authentic faith causes us to treat others with unconditional love and seriousness. Authentic Christianity should lead to maturity, character, and genuineness. Authenticity means we erase the gap between what we truly believe in our hearts and what we show to the world around us.

Today's challenge…begin modeling truth, the whole truth and nothing but the truth, so help us God. Meditate on truth. Speak truth. Confront with truth. Love truth. Seek truth. Walk in truth. May we be authentic Christians.

Day 72 The Final Authority

Your word have I hid in my heart that I might not sin against you.

Psalm 119:11

The first conviction we must have is that the Bible is the inspired and infallible Word of God and it is the final authority for our lives. How we clearly know and accurately recognize what Jesus is speaking to us is by dedicating ourselves to His Word.

The Bible is the criterion for truth and guards us from false philosophies and deceptions. Those who make no attempt to read and comprehend God's Word are susceptible to many voices other than His. Paul instructed Timothy, "Study to shew yourself approved unto God, a workman that needs not to be ashamed, rightly dividing the word of truth" (2 Timothy 2:15). We develop the mind of Christ within ourselves when we meditate on His Word.

If our Bible is falling apart, then our life never will! Whenever we seem to not have strength to carry on, we can find in Scripture the encouragement and power to take another step. Even when the world is living in fear, may we discover treasure in God's Word and find the courage we need.

Day 73 Keep Going

And Jesus said unto him, Go thy way; thy faith hath made thee whole. And immediately he received his sight, and followed Jesus in the way.

Mark 10:52

Blind Bartimaeus cried out and refused to be silenced when he heard that Jesus was passing by. Due to his faith and persistence, immediately he regained his sight and began following Jesus on the road. How much do we desire to receive the promises Jesus has placed in our hearts? Enough to push through those who would try to discourage us? Enough to keep doing His will even though it seems only bad things keep happening? Are we willing to press forward although every circumstance indicates the promises will not come to pass?

Refuse to be discouraged by what looks impossible. "...With God all things are possible" (Mark 10:27). May we be persistent in our pursuit of God's promise. Our greatest struggles often lead to our greatest triumphs. Difficult circumstances establish strong people in the end. Let us keep going!

Day 74 God is in Control

Remember the former things of old: for I am God, and there is none else; I am God, and there is none like me, Declaring the end from the beginning, and from ancient times the things that are not yet done, saying, My counsel shall stand, and I will do all my pleasure.

Isaiah 46:9–10

God is in control! If we could figure everything out for ourselves, then we could qualify as God's counselor. God does not need our counsel, rather we do need His. He desires our unfiltered love, complete loyalty, and fearless faith and trust.

Evidence of spiritual maturity is the inner confidence that Jesus is in control without our need to comprehend why He does things the way He does them. His ways are beyond human understanding: "For as the heavens are higher than the earth, so are my ways higher than your ways, and my thoughts than your thoughts" (Isaiah 55:9). Sometimes, it can be a blessing for Him not to answer our prayer. We may wonder why the relationship waned, the job fell through, or the business deal failed. We desire immediate gratification, yet God sees how current circumstances will impact our future. The best thing that could happen for us could be the reverse of what we desire to transpire at the time.

Jesus knows all and wants to work everything together for our good so we may live abundant lives of joy and love. Let us trust Him to bring the right opportunities and to protect us from harm. May we rest in His wisdom.

Day 75 Seeds of Growth

When his candle shined upon my head, and when by his light I walked through darkness.

Job 29:3

Each of us have walked through dark places in our lives—illnesses, broken relationships, loss of loved ones, or betrayal by those we love and trust. Discouragement during these times can cause us to feel like giving up. Nevertheless, God utilizes the dark situations to fulfill His divine purpose in us.

Jesus said, "Except a corn of wheat fall into the ground and die, it abides alone: but if it die, it brings forth much fruit" (John 12:24). We may not be aware of it, but buried in the darkness the seeds of our achievement are planted. In these dark times, we develop character and learn to trust the Lord and endure. We gain wisdom and mature in ways that we could not have obtained during the easier times of our lives.

The situations that appear to us as setbacks are the very things that propel us into deep spiritual growth. When we understand this, and accept it, the places of darkness and adversity become easier for us to bear.

Day 76 Speaking Life to Ourselves and Others

Death and life are in the power of the tongue: and they that love it shall eat the fruit thereof.

Proverbs 18:21.

Our words have the power to destroy and the power to build up. "A man shall be satisfied with good by the fruit of his mouth…" (Proverbs 12:14). What we speak has amazing influence or possibly even creative power over our lives.

If we say, "I'm so tired," we feel exhausted the entire day; or, saying "I fail at everything I attempt," we welcome discouragement and depression. We need to be careful about what we say because of the power our words have over us. It is imperative therefore that we begin each day by proclaiming blessings in our lives. "I am strong; I have God's favor; I have the ability to succeed; I am…" By speaking positive words of action and blessing we invite good things to happen for us.

"I am" are two of the most important words we can ever speak, because whatever we say after them can shape our reality. May every word that is ever spoken out of our mouths be words that lift up and never words that tear down, for ourselves and others. What we say is what we get!

Day 77 Our Help is in Jesus

Unless the Lord had been my help, my soul had almost dwelt in silence.

Psalm 94:17

Think about all the things we have gone through, some we feared we would never survive—breakups, unbearable problems, medical conditions, or deep loss, yet Jesus turned it around. He rescued us, enabled us to begin again, and gave us strength to move forward. These trials equipped us for our future and provided us a life story and history with the Lord.

Let go of what modern culture tells us that we should be and allow the Bible to give us direction for our lives. His Word can be encouragement for us daily. If we are in a difficult situation, we should reflect on how God helped and delivered us from past troubles and heartaches. By recalling the way Jesus protected, promoted, healed, and restored us, genuine faith arises within our heart and soul. We can then say, "Jesus, You made a way for me before and I know You will do it again. I trust that You are working all things together for my ultimate good."

Jesus knows how to turn things around. He will turn our sorrow into joy…if we simply let Him. Anytime we are distressed, dismayed, and heartbroken, anytime our plans are interrupted and our world is falling apart, just remember Jesus is ready and willing to share burdens too heavy to bear. May we, in faith, "Let Go and Let GOD" lead our way into a happier and brighter day.

Day 78 Soaring to New Heights

Now unto him that is able to do exceeding abundantly above all that we ask or think, according to the power that worketh in us.

Ephesians 3:20

People often limit themselves based on their family, friends, culture, lack of education, environment, social status, or past experiences. God does not want us to settle in a limited setting. He has big dreams and plans for us.

We have untapped potential just waiting to manifest itself. We have talents and gifts that can open new doors of opportunity. So stop making excuses for being stagnant or stuck. Even if we are in an environment of dysfunctionality, dependency, or misery, the wonderful news from Jesus is WE DO NOT HAVE TO STAY THERE!

When barriers obstruct our path, we can change our direction to reach our goals, yet we should never alter our motivation and determination to obtain our goals. Jesus wants us to know we can break through every limitation and soar to higher heights to achieve more than we can even imagine. This is a new day! With God, we can accomplish infinitely more than we can ask or think, exceeding abundantly more!

Day 79 Fearfully and Wonderfully Made

I have said, You are gods; and all of you are children of the most High.

Psalm 82:6

We frequently perceive what we do as who we are. However, our actions do not inevitably depict our identity. Who are we? We are children of the Most High God and Eternal Father! We are His children despite our faults, failures, or flaws. Realizing this increases our perceived value of ourselves.

What we do does not amend who we are and the value Jesus, our Creator, sees in us. We will never think of ourselves as being accepted by others until we first accept ourselves. The chief way to realize this is to strive for excellence in Christ first and also work toward excellence in each part of our lives daily. As we become more acceptable to ourselves, we will become increasingly acceptable to others.

"But you are a chosen generation, a royal priesthood, a holy nation, a peculiar people…" (I Peter 2:9). We are fearfully and wonderfully made by Jesus Christ!

Day 80 Prisoners of Hope

Turn you to the strong hold, you prisoners of hope: even today I do declare that I will render double unto you.

Zechariah 9:12

Being a prisoner means we are constrained by whatever has imprisoned us. According to this passage, we are "prisoners of hope." We cannot escape HOPE. We are held captive in a cell of hope for our soul by Jesus and His wonderful love!

Given all that we have been through, we should be dejected and discouraged. Despite all the forces that have been waged against us, we have faith that all will be well and that all is well with our souls. God will make a way somehow! Whether it is sickness, heartbreak, betrayal, or loss, nothing or no one can steal our hope in God. Our hope is not in doctors, experts, government or any other thing…only in God.

Let us follow what we believe rather than what we see and keep hoping in God. Jesus controls our destiny. We are prisoners of hope and He will restore double to us for all that we have lost. The hope He provides empowers us to see the light even when darkness surrounds us. Jesus promises to give us double of His goodness, favor, and all that relates to life and godliness. We are prisoners of Hope. Hallelujah!

Day 81 Learning to Forgive

Looking diligently lest any man fail of the grace of God; lest any root of bitterness springing up trouble you, and thereby many be defiled.

Hebrews 12:15

How we deal with feeling offended by others not only affects us, but it can also affect those close to us. We can choose to become angry and stressed anytime for most any reason. When we indulge or entertain negative emotions, we give something outside ourselves control over our happiness.

We should determine not to let trivial things upset us. As we begin to understand Jesus and His ways more fully, we become offended less and we react less to negative conditions. Instead, we look inwardly on how we can grow from the experience. The more anger we have in our hearts about the past, the less we are able to love in the present.

If we are offended by someone, we should reconcile readily with that person, if at all possible. Next, let us evaluate ourselves and be honest about our own failings. Only then, will we be able to forget our anger and walk in forgiveness and freedom.

Day 82 Liberty in the Holy Spirit

Now the Lord is that Spirit: and where the Spirit of the Lord is, there is liberty.

2 Corinthians 3:17

Today in the presence of Jesus, there is freedom, joy, peace, and refreshing. Our fresh start and new beginning awaits. Forget about failures and offenses of the past because negative thinking only upsets and delays our deliverance, productivity, and progress.

We refuse to allow our past to define us or to be imprisoned to it. Now is the time to leave the past in the past and move forward. God sees and is well aware of every offense, loss, and sin we have experienced. The wonderful thing about this is, for each of our setbacks, Jesus provides a comeback! For each regret, He provides a new beginning. For each sinful failure, He restores. For all the ashes of our lives, He gives beauty, and the oil of joy for our mourning.

"It is of the Lord's mercies that we are not consumed, because his compassions fail not. They are new every morning: great is thy faithfulness" (Lamentations 3:22-23). Live free in Jesus name!

Day 83 Enough

One of his disciples, Andrew, Simon Peter's brother, said unto him, There is a lad here, which has five barley loaves, and two small fishes: but what are they among so many?

John 6:8-9

A young boy had fives loaves and two fishes, yet Jesus used these to feed five thousand hungry people. God used what the lad made available to work a miracle!

Our resources are limited, yet God's are limitless. All that we could provide in the time of great need is meager until it is dedicated to Jesus. He then multiplies, empowers, enhances, enlarges, and increases so that it is sufficient to meet the need. We should bring what we have to do His work now, and not wait until we think we have enough to do what only He can do. We must stop waiting and wondering and bring Jesus what we have.

The talents and resources we have may seem insignificant when we try to compare them to what others around us possess. Yet, if we dedicate our life to the Lord, accept who we are, use what we have for His will in our lives, Jesus can do great and mighty things in us and through us. May we accept who we are and do what we can with all we have wherever we are and it will be enough for God to fulfill His plan through our lives. He can do more with us than we can.

Day 84 Anointed by God

Saying, Touch not mine anointed, and do my prophets no harm.

Psalm 105:15.

We are God's anointed ones! His anointing shields us when the enemy's attacks should have killed us. His anointing keeps our mind when everything seems to be going wrong. God's anointing gives us peace in the midst of the storm and keeps us safe from all harm.

This godly empowerment enables us to accomplish what we cannot do ourselves. The anointing enhances the talents and abilities we have, compensates for those which we do not possess, and helps us to conquer problems that seem impossible. Prayer, faith, and God's Word are the means through which the anointing flows.

Instead of murmuring and complaining about problems, declare today, "I am anointed of God and empowered by His Spirit. I can do all things through Christ Jesus!" Far too many Christians are attempting to run on adrenaline rather than the anointing. We should stop trying to accomplish everything on our own, with our own capabilities, strength, will, and intellect.

May we allow faith to arise and stir up the anointing Jesus has granted us, so we can do the things that we could not accomplish on our own. The anointing transforms us from sinners to saints, from average to more than conquerors, from rank strangers to a royal priesthood, and from unholy to the holiness of God.

Day 85 Beauty for Ashes

To appoint unto them that mourn in Zion, to give unto them beauty for ashes, the oil of joy for mourning, the garment of praise for the spirit of heaviness…

Isaiah 61:3

When setbacks and things we simply do not understand occur, it is easy for us to become discouraged. Life does not always seem fair, yet Jesus has promised that the things intended to cause us harm will eventually result in beneficial outcomes. He will give us "beauty for ashes."

In order to receive the beauty that Jesus wants to provide, we must let go of the ashes. May we let go of resentment and stop dwelling on the past, and keep pressing forward. We need to give Jesus the pain before we can receive the blessing, give Him the discouragement before we can obtain the oil of joy, and give Him the heaviness of our hearts in order to get the garment of praise. Before we can receive, we must first let go and cast all our cares upon Jesus.

Jesus wants to make a trade with us right now. Let us cast all our care on Him today, so He may give us beauty for our ashes.

No one ever cared for me like Jesus;

There's no other friend so kind as He.

No one else could take the sin and darkness from me;

O how much He cared for me (Charles Weigle).

Day 86 Learning to Let Go

Let all bitterness, and wrath, and anger, and clamor, and evil speaking, be put away from you, with all malice: And be kind one to another, tenderhearted, forgiving one another, even as God for Christ's sake has forgiven you.

Ephesians 4:31-32

Bitterness can easily creep into our lives from someone mistreating us, sickness, financial struggles, bad relationships, or numerous other situations. We cannot keep bad things from happening to us, but we can choose how we respond to them.

When we hold onto resentment and dwell on what caused it, we expose ourselves to becoming bitter. Hurt people have a tendency to hurt others when experiencing pain. The longer we dwell on it the deeper rooted the bitterness becomes on the inside. Bitterness poisons how we think and feel, where everything becomes prefaced with a negative attitude. It steals our joy, robs our peace, and destroys our ability to love and to feel loved.

Anytime things go wrong or people hurt us, let us be quick to forgive, release it readily and give it to Jesus. May we trust Him to defend us and to vindicate us. The truth is, until we let go, unless we forgive others and ourselves, we cannot move forward. When we forgive and let go, we heal and we grow.

Day 87 Look Up

My voice shall you hear in the morning, O Lord; in the morning will I direct my prayer unto you, and will look up.

Psalm 5:3

David prayed and then said, "I will look up," meaning I will wait expectantly. Prayer is more than making entreaties, more than offering praise, more than thanksgiving, and more than interceding for others. Prayer is not about our posture, whether we kneel, bow, stand, or lie down. Prayer is about humbling ourselves before the Lord. Prayer is believing that Jesus wants us there. Prayer is believing that He hears us and will act on our behalf in response to our prayers. Prayer is confidently and fervently expecting that Jesus will connect with us and will do whatever is best for us and those we care for.

After we have prayed we should look for God's favor and blessings all around us in everything we do and see. "Surely goodness and mercy shall follow me…" (Psalm 23:6). Jesus will bring to pass what He has promised us. OUR GOD IS FAITHFUL! We may have waited for a long time, yet deep in our hearts we have the blessed assurance that the answer is coming, our miracle that we have long awaited for is about to happen. "And let us not be weary in well doing: for in due season we shall reap, if we faint not" (Galatians 6:9).

Let us praise Jesus for meeting us in prayer today. We know that He always hears us and cares deeply about anything we share with Him. We will bless and praise Him for accepting us as His dear children.

Day 88 Pleasure in Prosperity

...Let the Lord be magnified, which has pleasure in the prosperity of his servant.

Psalm 35:27

Did you get that? God takes pleasure in prospering us! He wants us to form an abundant mindset. We progress toward what our mind continually meditates upon. If we constantly think on our lack and our struggle, our mind guides us toward feelings of defeat. Instead, we should think about how Jesus keeps His promises and never fails, and how He will make a way for us.

"This book of the law shall not depart out of your mouth; but you shall meditate therein day and night, that you may observe to do according to all that is written therein: for then you shall make your way prosperous, and then you shall have good success" (Joshua 1:8). Jesus will enable us to achieve levels that we could never have achieved without Him. He has a prosperous future in store as our soul prospers in His will.

We are children of the King of kings and Lord of lords! He wants us to be more successful than we even desire to be! Jesus takes pleasure in prospering us!

Day 89 Ruling Our Own Spirit

He that is slow to anger is better than the mighty; and he that rules his spirit than he that takes a city.

Proverbs 16:32

Self-control and patience are characteristics of a mature person equipped for success. Do we have enough self-control to not be moved by peer pressure? Are we patient in our difficult times? The Bible teaches us to rule our own spirit, but does not instruct us to rule over someone else's spirit.

Our toughest struggles help to build godly character. They create opportunities for us to grow and to exercise self-control and patience. We should use our struggles to improve ourselves and to draw nearer to Jesus. One of the main aspects of ruling our own spirit is not allowing adverse circumstances or negative people to get to us by causing us to feel discouraged or anxious.

Happiness, contentment, love, hope and gratitude are all choices we can make. Attitude is more important than our circumstances. Ruling our spirit reveals greatness. We can retain a cheerful countenance and a merry heart. Even though self-discipline is not the norm in our society any more, we should practice it.

A boat does not sink from water under it or surrounding it, rather, it can only sink when water gets inside. Today, may we make up our minds that nothing gets inside us but faith, peace, love, and a "can do" positive mindset.

Day 90 A Victorious Mindset

For though we walk in the flesh, we do not war after the flesh: (For the weapons of our warfare are not carnal, but mighty through God to the pulling down of strongholds;) Casting down imaginations, and every high thing that exalts itself against the knowledge of God, and bringing into captivity every thought to the obedience of Christ.

2 Corinthians 10:3-5

Satan will try to take our failures and offenses to build strongholds in our lives. If he can fill our minds with negativity and a defeatist mentality, we will lose. We should determine in our minds not to live our lives in fear, feeling our problems are so big we cannot conquer them.

"The only thing we have to fear is fear itself" (Franklin Roosevelt). God's Word makes an even bolder promise, we have nothing to fear, period! Having nothing to fear does not mean we will have no struggles. What it does mean is that nothing has the power to dominate or cripple our lives—fear of failure, fear of the future, or fear of anything else. Much of how we become who we are and what we are is by what we think. We can change who we are and what we are by changing the way we think.

May we maintain a victorious mindset, realizing that Jesus has provided us with the spiritual arsenal we need to tear down every satanic stronghold. May we realize beyond the shadow of any doubt that We CAN DO all things through Christ Jesus!

Day 91 Listen

My sheep hear my voice, and I know them, and they follow me.

John 10:27

Communication is an interactive loop between two or more parties and is essential to building strong relationships. Listening is a vital element to successful communication. Did you know that "listen" contains the same letters as "silent?" We draw closer to Jesus and build a more intimate relationship with Him in prayer by listening to Him through His Word, by being sensitive to each unction of the Spirit, and by receiving godly counsel from others who know Him well. "Wisdom is the reward you get for a lifetime of listening when you would have rather talked" (Mark Twain).

God often speaks in the silence of our hearts and listening to Him is the best beginning to prayer. We miss far too much when we listen to carnality or fear rather than listening to Jesus. Obedience to God is listening to Him and having an open heart and a determined will to follow the path He has prepared for us. "To the top of Amana, to the dens of lions, or to the hills of leopards, we will follow our Beloved. Precious Jesus, draw us, and we will run after thee" (Charles Spurgeon).

Day 92 Be Still

…For he that wavers is like a wave of the sea driven with the wind and tossed.

James 1:6

In the midst of this unpredictable world, we occasionally feel hopeful and then fearful, encouraged and then discouraged. Sometimes it seems difficult to maintain unwavering faith. This is why we must remain focused on Jesus and trust Him, the Author and Finisher of our faith. With God all things are possible!

Today, we should take a few minutes to slip away from the chaos in our world and connect with Jesus. Be still. Take some time in which to remember, stop, take a breath, and be aware that He is right here, right now. Let us carry this realization with us as we ease back into our day. May we determine to put Jesus first, to spend time talking to Him and to know and experience more of Him. When we start our day in His presence, everything else seems more manageable and we will feel balanced. Peace fills the atmosphere when we slow down and experience God's presence.

Throughout this day, let us maintain an ongoing communication with Jesus, thanking Him for all His blessings and for everyone He has placed in our lives. May our minds to be still and rest in His presence.

Day 93 Praying for Our Enemies

For if you forgive men their trespasses, your Heavenly Father will also forgive you.

Matthew 6:14

How can we even dare to go before God and ask Him to forgive us if we refuse to forgive others? The mercy of Jesus is to be shared! If we do not share His mercy, we will lose the blessing of it. We have been forgiven to share forgiveness.

Forgiveness opens the heart for our soul to heal. However, forgiving does not mean we allow people to continue mistreating us nor do we avoid confronting their bad behavior. It does mean we release the anger and vengefulness, and leave it in the capable hands of Jesus to defend us. Daily, our mindfulness of God's mercy should help us to renew forgiveness in our own lives by forgiving others first before we ask Jesus to forgive us.

Applying forgiveness even enables us to pray compassionately for those who have caused us pain. Jesus instructs us to "love your enemies and pray for those who persecute you" (Matthew 5:44). The word love in this context is to "rescue from hate," for both us and our enemies. Having the desire to forgive is evidence we are being children of God who desire to free others from their sin and bless them with mercy and grace.

We will find it very difficult to forgive, if we do not first pray for our enemies. Praying for them can trigger the healing and genuine forgiveness we need. If we choose to forgive, we will be forgiven by God.

Day 94 Pure in Heart

Blessed are the pure in heart: for they shall see God.

Matthew 5:8

A pure heart is required for true, authentic worship. Much of human life is tainted by duplicity and deception. Pure motives and an unspoiled heart are of utmost importance if we are to live the life of the kingdom and family of God. The context for the word "pure" in this verse is to cleanse, liberate, or purify. Jesus is informing us that when we cleanse and purify ourselves from life's impurities, or anything that taints our sanctified relationship with Him, we will be blessed.

Our hearts can be dishonest and selfish. Sin, bitterness, fear, and doubt are a few of the contaminates that often affect or "infect" us. We need to let go immediately of any and all of these poisons, that they be no longer toxic to our hearts. Genuine prayer gives us a pure heart. Rather than being concerned about having the right words, we should be more concerned about having the right heart. It is not eloquence that God seeks from our prayer…just honesty.

May Jesus cleanse our hearts with His Spirit and continually dwell within us until He catches us away into Heaven to abide with Him eternally. May our lives demonstrate our faithfulness to Him, letting Him guard our hearts from impurity, deceitfulness, and selfishness. May Jesus help us as we attempt to be pure in heart!

Day 95 Forgive Anyway

Then said Jesus, Father, forgive them; for they know not what they do…

Luke 23:34

The amazing and powerful love and forgiveness of Jesus is astounding! Who else could voice such words of understanding and forgiveness for the very people crucifying Him? He was correct in saying, "they know not what they do." Although those who betrayed, falsely accused, mocked, hated, and crucified Jesus did not ask for His forgiveness, He forgave them anyway. Jesus gave us an example on how to release bitterness from our lives. Can we look behind the words and actions of those who have wronged us, as Jesus did, and see their brokenness and despair? Can we meet their hate with love? Harboring unforgiveness is like drinking poison and hoping it will kill our enemies. Those who refuse to forgive reveal that they are weak and insecure. The strong in faith who are secure in their relationship with Jesus readily forgive those who wrong them.

Let us look beneath the hard exterior into the wounded hearts of our offenders. May we look with God's eyes, opening our hearts to forgiveness and love. We do not simply forgive for our offender's benefit. We need to forgive in order to help ourselves too. Although the world was harsh to Jesus, He spoke forgiveness over all His accusers, abusers, and mockers. Even though He had the power to crush them, He chose to forgive them. Jesus did it for love, a love we have received and now must share.

Day 96 Testing Times, Better Days are Coming

My brethren, count it all joy when you fall into divers temptations; Knowing this, that the trying of your faith works patience.

James 1:2-3

Our testing times often last longer, sometimes much longer, than we anticipated. It is easy to become discouraged and begin murmuring and complaining. However, Jesus wants us to look to Him for strength to get through the days and to ask Him for wisdom to learn from the experiences.

Testing times try our faith in order to shape our character. These are different than temptations. Temptations do not come from the Lord, yet tests draw us nearer to Him. If we reflect over our lives of the times we felt closest to Jesus, we would realize that it was during the most difficult times that we became highly sensitive to His presence and felt Him so near.

Jesus wants us to spiritually mature to the point where we keep our faith regardless of our circumstances. Testing times are temporary and will not always last. We should keep our eyes and hearts on Jesus and never lose hope. He will sustain us and help us to become complete in Him. May we hold tightly to Him during the tough times, so we can consider it "all joy." Better days are coming, if not in this life, then most definitely in the next one!

Day 97 Purpose-Driven Life

Let your eyes look right on, and let your eyelids look straight before you.

Proverbs 4:25

To fulfill the destiny that Jesus has for us, we need to comprehend our divine purpose. "If you don't know where you are going, any road will get you there" (Lewis Carroll). We need goals, the right plan, and then work toward these each day. Today's verse cautions us to keep our eyes fixed directly ahead, not looking off to the right nor to the left. In other words, we should not waste time and energy on things which are not pleasing to God which could hinder us from reaching our destiny.

In order to get started in the right direction, we need to pray in the Spirit and ask Jesus for His guidance and wisdom toward setting our plans and schedule to accomplish His will in our lives. He has promised the Holy Spirit to lead and guide us, "Howbeit when he, the Spirit of truth, is come, he will guide you into all truth…and he will shew you things to come" (John 16:13). We may have felt at times that we were being dragged through hell. The battle, however, helped bring us back to life and our purpose kept us in alignment with Heaven.

Walking in God's will is not always easy, yet it is the most joyful and exciting life one could live. He will abundantly bless all we do as long as we walk according to His will and His plan. May Jesus help us to stay properly focused and structure our days to walk in our God-given purpose.

Day 98 Table of Blessing

You prepare a table before me in the presence of my enemies: you anoint my head with oil; my cup runs over.

Psalm 23:5

Occasionally, we are tempted to flee from a setting where we encounter ridicule and antagonism, yet we do not have to leave it to be blessed. Jesus will bless us right where we are, even in the midst of our enemies.

God promotes us in these environments as a means to vindicate us so our antagonists will know that, even if they do not accept us, Jesus is with us. Our outlook of negative people and situations should be reframed accordingly, "My enemies may be mocking me now, but their opposition is making the path for God to promote me." Jesus is loyal and faithful.

May we move onward with a new vision and courage to realize that we cannot be defeated because our God is with us. He will go before us and prepare the way for blessings. Jesus will open new doors of opportunity. Even if the promise is delayed, we know it will come. Let us come boldly to the table of the Lord and receive all the blessings He has prepared—love, strength, health, opportunity, and so much more.

Day 99 Watch Our Words

You are snared with the words of your mouth, you are taken with the words of your mouth.

Proverbs 6:2

Our words have unrecognized power. They can produce faith or fear. The words we speak can ensnare us, cause us to stumble, and hinder us from our divine purpose and potential. However, the words we speak can also liberate us, encourage us, and help us to achieve our destiny.

Each of us deal with negative thoughts trying to fill our minds, but they are minimally effective until we verbalize them. We give them power when we speak them. If "I can't" is a frequent phrase in our vocabulary, we limit our potential each time we say it. We should stay alert to this, for our thoughts become our words; our words become our actions; our actions become our habits; our habits become our character; and, our character becomes our destiny.

We conquer negative thoughts by focusing on the promises of Jesus rather than on our problems and by speaking life-giving words. "I can do ALL THINGS through Christ who empowers, enriches, equips, enlightens, energizes, recreates, revives, promotes, strengthens, purifies, sponsors, and prepares me! Yes, I can...ALL THINGS, I can!" (Israelmore Ayivor).

Day 100 Give Jesus The Broken Pieces

The Lord is nigh unto them that are of a broken heart; and saves such as be of a contrite spirit.

Psalm 34:18

Each of us have had our hearts broken before by betrayal and have experienced shame, fear, or rejection. God feels our pain. He hurts when we hurt. Jesus wants us to know that He comes nearer to us in our times of brokenness.

Although brokenness may not seem like a pleasant experience, it yields tremendous deliverance and restoration with God. Our carnal nature is brought under subjection, and unnecessary sinful attributes are discarded, so that Christ-like nature radiates in and from us. We become sensitized to God's voice and direction for our lives. David said, "...I am like a broken vessel" (Psalm 31:12). Yet, through his brokenness he developed into a man after God's own heart.

May God enable us to allow our brokenness to bring healing and freedom and the ability to help guide others to Him. Jesus will mend our broken hearts if we will give Him all the pieces. God uses broken vessels to bring good into the world.

Day 101 Listening in the Silence

…A time to keep silence, and a time to speak.

Ecclesiastes 3:7

After Elijah had prophesied to King Ahab, the wicked King of Israel, the Lord instructed Elijah to hide in the brook of Cherith (see I Kings 17). For three and a half years he was silent, prophesying to nobody and only seeking God before eventually going forward to do mighty works. The path to true intimacy with God is an inward one, where we enter into His glorious presence through the quietness of our souls.

Silence in our lives is not an indication that Jesus is not working on our behalf. Although He is preparing the conditions, most importantly, He is changing us. God uses the silence to mold us and to shape our character. We grow in spiritual maturity and obtain strength and experience that we will need to fulfill our divine destiny.

Instead of resisting the silence, realize that it is vital for us to add depth to our spiritual life. Our mission will eventually be revealed! "How rare it is to find a soul quiet enough to hear God speak" (Francois Fenelon). Before we pray, let us be silent first and worship Jesus in His presence. Meditate on all He is able to do and the way He delights for us to seek Him.

Day 102 Step Out on Faith

And it shall come to pass, as soon as the soles of the feet of the priests that bear the ark of the Lord, the Lord of all the earth, shall rest in the waters of Jordan, that the waters of Jordan shall be cut off from the waters that come down from above; and they shall stand upon an heap.

Joshua 3:13

As the priests dared to step into the unfamiliar and unknown, the waters of Jordan began to roll back. We think we can wait to go and do after Jesus has moved the mountain or parted the waters for us. Jesus, however, wants us to go and do, then He will move the mountain and part the waters for us.

We say, "When my bills are all paid, when I have enough, when my children are grown, I'll go." God says, "Go and I will provide for you and make a way." Jesus expects for us to step out in faith first. God continually places us in situations that seem impossible. If we will step out in faith, frequently into the unknown, when God says "go" or "do," the right doors will open, the right people will come to us. Vision and maturity usually are birthed from adversity and struggle, by stepping away from what is comfortable and familiar and stepping out into the unknown.

May our minds be filled with confident thoughts and may we learn to keep stepping out on faith. Jesus wants to part the Jordan waters of our lives, but we must take the first step.

Day 103 Disciplined to Friendship with Jesus

Now no chastening for the present seems to be joyous, but grievous: nevertheless afterward it yields the peaceable fruit of righteousness unto them which are exercised thereby.

Hebrews 12:11

The original Greek word used for "chastening" in this verse means "discipline." No one enjoys discipline. However, we must apply it to our lives daily in order to live righteously and to accomplish God's will.

The temptation to gossip, to be slothful, or to "let someone have it!" may have strong appeal at times. Yet, lack of discipline to do right in difficult circumstances hinders our growth and development and it can land us in trouble. More often than not, discipline requires saying "no" to things. Each time we yield to temptation our carnal nature becomes stronger. However, every time we resist it and remain disciplined to God's will, we grow in maturity and wisdom, plus we experience new levels of freedom and favor in Jesus.

We should not only discipline ourselves to resist the bad stuff, we must also be disciplined to doing good. Spiritual discipline helps us to become more like Jesus, daily doing the right things to develop our Christian journey. Spiritual disciplines are invaluable to feeling closer to God.

A disciplined life leads to happiness and an undisciplined life leads to suffering. May we discipline ourselves so God does not have to.

Day 104 Loving Our Enemies

… I say unto you, Love your enemies, bless them that curse you, do good to them that hate you, and pray for them which despitefully use you, and persecute you.

Matthew 5:44

Loving the unlovable is something we all have difficultly doing. Our natural instinct is to protect ourselves from them. We have no problem being good to those who treat us well. Yet, when someone mistreats us we can easily become resentful, bitter, vengeful, and speak ill of them. Jesus cautions us to love and to bless them, more for our sake than for their sake.

The forgiveness and compassion we show others is directly correlated with God's mercy and compassion toward us. Life is too short to live it bitterly. Bitterness imprisons, love liberates. "As we pour out our bitterness, God pours in His peace" (F.B. Meyer). Loving our enemies should be a blessing rather than a burden. We experience glorious freedom and our enemies no longer control our feelings toward them when we choose love over bitterness.

Loving our enemies is a wonderful gift from Jesus, which enables us to love Him deeper. Each time we determine to love our enemy, we realize anew that Jesus loved us enough to give His life for us, even when we were unlovable (see Romans 5:10). "We may not be able to prevent other people from being our enemies, but we can prevent ourselves from being enemies toward others" (Warren Wiersbe). Let us release our offenders in Jesus name, and the Lord will make us whole and take us to new levels in Him.

Day 105 It is Finished!

When Jesus therefore had received the vinegar, he said, It is finished: and he bowed his head, and gave up the ghost.

John 19:30

Words have power. As Jesus hung on the cross with His last few remaining breaths, He cried, "It is finished!" These three words changed everything!

These powerful words altered the course of our lives forever! The stranglehold of darkness and defeat over hearts and minds of people was over. He was bringing to an end those things that were keeping us from Him and our divine destiny. Regardless of what we are facing today or what we have had to endure, we will win for it is finished. At the foot of the cross is a fresh start and a new beginning, a place to bring to an end the guilt, sin, and depression that may have been negatively impacting our lives. Our debt has been paid, strongholds are broken, and we are free!

Because of what Jesus has done, His favor is now upon us and we can rise above our past and our current circumstances to greatness. It is settled. It is over. It is done. It is paid in full. IT IS FINISHED!

Day 106 The Transformation Process

Therefore if any man be in Christ, he is a new creature: old things are passed away; behold, all things are become new.

2 Corinthians 5:17

Satan continually tries to remind us of all the mistakes we have made because he wants us to live in guilt and condemnation. The very instant we turn sincerely to Jesus and repent of our sins we are cleansed and forgiven. We cannot change the past, yet we can do better going forward. We are not perfect, but we are forgiven. So, the time has come to release the guilt and forgive ourselves.

When we accept Jesus Christ as our Lord and Savior, we trade our old life for a new one. As we become full of the Holy Spirit a transformation process starts. He strips away the old habits and thoughts and replaces them with freedom and truth. We trade sin for forgiveness, pride for humility, fear for love, weakness for strength, and sadness for joy.

Though Jesus works the transformation process in our lives, we are to surrender each area and live obedient to His will in order to achieve fullness in Him. May we consider each morning as a fresh start and a new beginning.

Day 107 Excellent Living

And whatsoever you do, do it heartily, as to the Lord, and not unto men.

Colossians 3:23

Jesus wants us to live a life of excellence, which means pursuing and doing the best we can with the gifts and abilities He has given us. A person of excellence is never satisfied with doing things halfway or just enough to get by.

Mediocrity is rampant in our world, but this is not God's will for us. He will bless us and make a way if we will do our best even when others do not notice it. After we have experienced excellent living, we cannot be content with mediocrity. We should do all things enthusiastically as unto the Lord. One way to easily make this our common practice is to treat everything we do as worship to the Lord. If we always do our best, we can take comfort in knowing that Jesus notices what we do and He will reward our faithfulness.

We do what we do for Jesus, not for people. Let us determine to be individuals of excellence from this day forward by doing ordinary things extraordinarily well. Besides, if we do things right to begin with, we will not have to do them over.

Day 108 Our Protector

...Touch not mine anointed, and do my prophets no harm.

Psalm 105:15

When people attack or slander God's anointed, they are fighting against God. Wonderfully and amazingly, His anointed need not to fight these battles using their own efforts. Jesus is our Protector. We can fearlessly and courageously "stand still, and see the salvation of the Lord" (Exodus 14:13).

Christ in us is greater than the forces attempting to defeat us. His blessings are greater than betrayal, detrimental words spoken against us, and those who try to tear down our reputation. Nothing and no one can remove the Lord's blessing from us. We are blessed regardless of the words of others and our circumstances. Nobody gives God's blessings to us and nobody can take them away. This joy, love, and peace that we have within, the world didn't give to us, so the world can't take it away.

Our protection comes in our nearness to Jesus, not in the distance from our enemies. The safest place to live is in God's divine will, and the safest protection is the name of Jesus. Let us slip away quietly into the safe haven of His loving presence today.

Day 109 The Pain of Pruning

...Every branch that bears fruit, he purges it, that it may bring forth more fruit.

John 15:2

There are times when we have so many things encumbering our lives that God cannot reach us. Our daily responsibilities may seem good and productive, while our spiritual fruit is dying on the vine. Jesus periodically prunes us so we can grow richly and bear healthy fruit in our lives. When He does this, we sometimes wonder why He slowed our progress, removed certain individuals from us or instigated such a setback. God prunes us at just the right time, even though it may not seem that way to us. The pruning process is usually painful, yet it makes us heathier in our spiritual walk and increases our ability to produce good fruit (see Galatians 5:22-23). It additionally prepares us to receive greater than if we had not gone through the experience.

Life's greatest lessons are learned through pain. The intensity of our pain signifies the escalation of our future. Perhaps this is a good day to start self-pruning from social media and other things that waste our time. Are unproductive activities stealing our spiritual development and sensitivity to God's voice or keeping us from spending quality time improving family relationships? Let us ask Jesus for help today in recognizing the fruitless things in our lives. May He give us discernment to understand the timing and the courage to pursue the right changes to make.

Day 110 Intentionally Being Still with Jesus

Be still, and know that I am God…

Psalm 46:10

God instructs us to release and to be still. In our busy lives, it can be tough to find stillness and serenity. Even if we discover it externally, it is still a challenge internally, because our minds are so busy.

We become frustrated when we try to change things or people that only God is able to change. We get upset because they do not do what we think they should do or become discouraged that things did not work out the way we had planned. We get irritated anytime we try to be God in trying to repair or manage everything and everybody. The major problem for us is that we perceive being still with the Lord as inactivity. Jesus wants us to realize when we are intentionally still, we can hear His voice and become much more aware of His presence.

In His stillness the world seems smaller, Jesus appears greater, and it becomes easier for us to follow our divine purpose rather than our own carnal path. May we release the pressure issues in our lives to Jesus and bask in His presence. Let us set aside a few minutes this day to be still before the Lord and to listen for His voice.

Day 111 Be a Praiser Not a Complainer

And when the people complained, it displeased the Lord…

Numbers 11:1

Most people would not view murmuring and complaining as sin, yet it is. We can indirectly find fault and murmur against the Lord about circumstances and people who He has allowed to enter our lives. Continual griping and complaining displeases God. Like the Israelites, we are prone to complain rather than thanking the Lord for the victory He has promised. We can waste far too much time and energy complaining. Those who complain the most accomplish the least.

Why is complaining bad? For one, it focuses on the problem rather than looking for a solution. Secondly, it repels people who could help us. Thirdly, it discounts the probable way God is working in our struggles and crises to bring improvement in our lives. Lastly, complaining keeps the complainer mired in personal sorrow and pain.

Even if we are unable to remove irritations in our lives, we can decide to change our thought processes about them. By focusing on being grateful to Jesus and praising Him for all He has done, we will experience higher levels of contentment and possess inner joy and peace. Gratitude releases God's blessings and moves Him to intervene on our behalf.

Instead of complaining about the way things are, let us do something to change them. Let us "enter into His gates with thanksgiving, and into His courts with praise. Be thankful to Him, and bless His name" (Psalm 100:4). Rather than allowing ourselves to be complainers, let us be praisers!

Day 112 The Golden Rule

And as you would that men should do to you, do you also to them likewise.

Luke 6:31

We often feel like no one really understands us or what we are going through, and that they just don't get us. The important thing to remember in the midst of these feelings is to make sure that we still treat others good and respectfully. If people do not treat us good, we may have a tendency to be rude or hurtful toward them in return or even have misplaced aggression toward others.

In today's verse, Jesus instructs us to treat people the way we desire to be treated by them. If we enjoy being treated nicely, then treat others nicely. If we feel ignored or left out, let us find someone to include or to bring into our circle. If we compliment and encourage those around us, they will enjoy our presence and we will be influential in their lives. When we choose joy and share it with others, our joy multiplies each time we share it.

Each of us can improve someone's life today with a touch, a smile, a kind word, a listening ear, a sincere compliment, or the tiniest deed of caring. Let us be intentional in loving others. Everyone loves to be loved.

Day 113 Resurrection Day

. . . I am the resurrection, and the life: he that believes in me, though he were dead, yet shall he live.

John 11:25

What an amazing and powerful promise! Though these physical bodies die, we shall live on and never die! Romans 6 informs us that when we are baptized, we die to sin and share in the death and resurrection of Jesus. Our lives become fused with His. His future is our future! His victory is our victory! His resurrection is our resurrection!

Jesus died and rose again so we could be free, free from any and all evil bondages, free from sin, free from depression, free from wrath, free from negativity, and so much more. We are made in the image of our Heavenly Father. Each of us have seeds of greatness. We were created to live free, to be joyful, to fulfill our divine purpose. Because of Jesus, we are destined to soar!

The time for us to allow Jesus to free us from any spiritual shackles that have us bound is now. He came to liberate us. Our Almighty God is working in our lives even now. Receive it in Jesus name! Resurrection Day is our Independence Day!

Day 114 Scars of Our Testimony

But he was wounded for our transgressions, he was bruised for our iniquities: the chastisement of our peace was upon him; and with his stripes we are healed.

Isaiah 53:5

We all have hidden scars from wounds of our past. They may be from something someone did, a broken relationship, mistakes made, or a tremendous loss. We frequently try to conceal the scars because they remind us of the pain. The scars of Jesus similarly reveal His unfailing love for us. They remind us that He understands all that we have been through.

It is sobering, yet enlightening, to consider that Jesus willingly took our place. "Greater love has no man than this, that a man lay down his life for his friends" (John 15:13). Jesus showed the greatest love of all and it was for us!

We can have peace with the scars. Our scars are part of our testimony, relaying our story of where Jesus has brought us from and how He has changed and improved our lives. They reveal where Satan tried to destroy us, yet Jesus saved, healed, and delivered us…just in time!

Day 115 Inner Promptings

Trust in the Lord with all thine heart; and lean not unto thine own understanding. In all your ways acknowledge him, and he shall direct your paths.

Proverbs 3:5-6

Verse five of today's passage warns us to not lean on our own understanding. A plethora of information passes through our minds continuously. This is where Satan will constantly try to attack us and convince us of his lies, which are contradictory to the infallible truths of God's Word. We must be cautious not to rely on our own instincts and feelings, but to follow scriptural guidance and the promptings of the Holy Spirit.

We must learn to discern when Jesus is speaking to us. Usually it is a gentle inner prompting that we need to do something or go somewhere. At other times we may sense a disturbance inwardly in which something just does not seem right, and we know to stay away. This is the Lord trying to protect us. We should remember that Spirit promptings will always align with Scripture.

May we never ignore or dismiss our inner spiritual promptings. Stay alert and allow the Holy Spirit and Scripture to guide and protect us. "Howbeit when he, the Spirit of truth, is come, he will guide you into all truth…" (John 16:13).

Day 116 Humility Conquers Pride

Talk no more so exceeding proudly; let not arrogance come out of your mouth…

I Samuel 2:3

Regardless of our accomplishments and abilities we should remain humble and meek, for pride goes before destruction and an arrogant spirit before a fall. After all, it was pride that changed Satan from an angel into a devil. Nothing distinguishes us from Satan more than being humble.

"Humility is not thinking less of yourself, it's thinking of yourself less" (C. S. Lewis). Being humble does not mean we think little of ourselves, thinking we are nothing, rather it is being wholly dependent on God for all in every situation. Humility is the by-product of being with Jesus.

The Bible tells us that we cannot do everything on our own. The best way to view our world is through a scriptural lens which informs us that we are not great, but Jesus is! When we have this view, we can deal with pride effectively. Some ways we can conquer pride is to become accountable to someone, center our attention on God and His will rather than ourselves, pray in the Spirit, and walk in obedience to His Word.

May God reveal pride in our lives and enable us to humble ourselves by the power of the Holy Spirit. May He grant us more of His grace and favor, and help us to love better.

Day 117 God's Masterpiece

For we are his workmanship, created in Christ Jesus unto good works, which God has before ordained that we should walk in them.

Ephesians 2:10

We were created by God. Therefore, He informs us of the true reason for why we exist and what we were designed to do. Jesus gives us purpose. If we try to function outside our purpose for existing, our life becomes confusing and extremely difficult. Furthermore, our worth should not be based on what others think of us, what we have achieved, or all that we possess. Our worth should be built exclusively on the fact that we are children of the Most High God. We have royalty within.

The way others treat us does not change our value or importance. Nothing we do, nothing we attain, and nothing we overcome can make us more precious. We are valuable now! We are fearfully and wonderfully made by God. We are His workmanship, His masterpiece!

May we walk with confidence, realizing we are children of the King of kings and Lord of lords! "I will praise you; for I am fearfully and wonderfully made…" (Psalm 139:14).

Day 118 Remove the Mask

And he said unto me, My grace is sufficient for you: for my strength is made perfect in weakness. Most gladly therefore will I rather glory in my infirmities, that the power of Christ may rest upon me.

2 Corinthians 12:9

We are all guilty of putting on a good front, appearing to be "fine," even when we are really struggling. Confidence is wonderful, but wearing a mask of pretense can be unhealthy. We fear that, if someone sees our weakness, our image will suffer. Jesus will not bless the pretentious mask. He will only bless our authenticity.

There is amazing power, freedom, and release available in openness and sincerity. When we pour ourselves out to Jesus, He will fill and empower us with His Spirit. We should humble ourselves in His presence today, stop the masquerade, so Jesus can help us grow and develop properly. Jesus will use our weakness to open our eyes to discovering His strength. Our weakness is an open door for His endless mercy, grace, and power to flow into our lives.

Jesus is simply waiting for us to humble ourselves enough to open the door to our hearts. He will meet us with open arms where we are right now and heal our wounds, if we will only let Him.

Day 119 Heal Our Land

If my people, which are called by my name, shall humble themselves, and pray, and seek my face, and turn from their wicked ways; then will I hear from heaven, and will forgive their sin, and will heal their land.

2 Chronicles 7:14

Much more than we realize, our world is reliant on Christians' relationship with Jesus. No political party, government, or institution can truly save us. Real change comes solely by the life-changing power of Jesus Christ in people's hearts.

God is longing for us to humble ourselves in prayer, to turn from any and all wickedness, and to intercede for our nation and our world. The healing of our land begins with the healing of ourselves. "But we have this treasure in earthen vessels…" (2 Corinthians 4:7). We are the earthen vessels, the land in which Christ dwells. We become whole by humbling ourselves in prayerful repentance regarding any sin or evil in our lives, and by forsaking the sin and turning to Jesus with all our hearts. Furthermore, we can trust Him to mend our families, friends, co-workers, and other individuals in our lives.

Crises in our world can be a wake-up call that Jesus is sovereign and that we should endlessly be in a state of repentance humbly seeking His favor. May we rise up and shine the light of Jesus until the darkness is gone!

Day 120 Healed to Help Others

For I am poor and needy, and my heart is wounded within me.

Psalm 109:22

In the Old Testament, priests were not allowed to go into the holy place to minister if they were sick or had visible cuts or sores. A great number of Christians are attempting to help others heal, while they themselves are still wounded or emotionally bleeding internally. This does not mean that if we are not completely whole we should not minister to others. What it does mean is, if we ourselves are whole, we will more effectively bring healing to others.

How can we minister freedom from addiction or emotional hurt to others if we are in bondage to addiction or are still suffering from emotional scars. Jesus delights greatly in using people who have been healed of their wounds to bring healing to others.

May we run to our Heavenly Father today and ask Him to heal any brokenness so we can be made whole. Then He can effectively use us to heal others. "The most eloquent prayer is the prayer through hands that heal and bless" (Billy Graham).

Day 121 Godly Character

A good man out of the good treasure of his heart brings forth that which is good…

Luke 6:45

Jesus is more concerned with the condition of our heart and soul than with our outward appearance and possessions (see I Peter 3:3-4). We frequently spend an overabundance of time on our appearance each day, making certain that we look just right, much more than we spend developing our character, preparing positive thoughts and forming the right attitudes. Although we should dress nice and take care of our possessions, having godly character is vital, because our attitude will dictate our behavior and actions.

Our character can be determined more by the lack of certain experiences than by those we have had. "Be more concerned with your character than your reputation, because your character is what you really are, while your reputation is merely what others think you are" (John Wooden).

Today, we should focus our hearts and minds correctly by first clearing our conscience of any wrong we may have committed and seeking forgiveness from the Lord. Let us forgive anyone who may have offended us and release any fears or concerns to God. If we do this, we will be an encouragement and shining light to everyone we interact with throughout our day.

Day 122 Believe Within and Receive Without

As a man thinks in his heart, so is he…

Proverbs 23:7

We can become addicted to having problems. Our entire life can appear to revolve around our problems and even become identified with them. We can allow the problems to influence all we do and everything we say.

Albert Einstein said, "We cannot solve our problems with the same thinking we used when we created them." We should not permit ourselves to fall into the temptation of allowing problems to control our thinking and rule every conversation we may have. Let us refuse to permit our lives to be taken over by our problems. Let us make a promise to Jesus, from this time forward, we determine not to waste anymore of our valuable time feeling sorry for ourselves or wallowing in self-pity over circumstances we cannot change. We should also determine to stop using our problems as a crutch in our lives. Determine to live each day to the fullest, anticipating all the wonderful things Jesus has in store as we follow Him.

All we need to do is believe. One touch of the favor of God can bring our hopes to pass. However, we must see it on the inside before this can ever come to pass on the outside.

Day 123 Get Untangled

Stand fast therefore in the liberty wherewith Christ has made us free, and be not entangled again with the yoke of bondage.

Galatians 5:1

Our lives often feel like we are tangled up in knots, one problem after another, with no progress being made, and that we are going utterly nowhere. During such times, we should consider that, although we may have far to go, we have come a long way from where we were and from who we used to be.

We constantly hope for a simple fix, the one easy change that will erase our problems with a simple stroke. Barely anything in life works this way. Success, however, necessitates making numerous tiny steps, one after the other, doing right, staying disciplined, and avoiding irresponsible missteps. The key is to thank Jesus for the progress we have made to this point, to stay focused, and to trust Him to guide us to our ultimate day-to-day freedom.

Our freedom in Jesus Christ does not mean we are free to live as we want. It does mean we have the freedom to live as we ought. We are led by His Spirit and governed by His Word. We live clothed in Christ's righteousness. This is true freedom! Let us proclaim our freedom today and be strong in Him.

Day 124 Love Never Fails

And now abides faith, hope, charity, these three; but the greatest of these is charity.

1 Corinthians 13:13

The Greek word used for "charity" in the Bible's love chapter is "agapē," which is the supernatural and unconditional love of God. Spiritual maturity is not necessarily determined by how long we have been a Christian, but rather in how we behave toward people.

The foundation for us to demonstrate unconditional love and kindness for others is the forgiveness and love that Jesus has shown us (see Colossians 3:13). Are we kind to our family and co-workers? What about people at the checkout counters, servers at restaurants, or those who cut us off in traffic? Agapē is not based on emotions or feelings, but on an act of our will. God's love is key to having a successful marriage and genuine friendships. We decide to walk in love even when we do not feel like loving.

Having Jesus fill us with His supernatural love enables us to become what we were destined to become. May God make us vessels of His divine love, loving others the way He loves us. Love never fails!

Day 125 Guided by Scripture and Loved by God

All scripture is given by inspiration of God, and is profitable for doctrine, for reproof, for correction, for instruction in righteousness: That the man of God may be perfect, thoroughly furnished unto all good works.

2 Timothy 3:16-17

Bible Scripture is God-breathed! This means His life is in every scriptural promise and we have all we will ever need to complete our divine purpose through His Word!

Scripture motivates and keeps us on the right path in our calling. His Word is not to beat ourselves and others over the head with; but rather, it is to help us become our best for Jesus. Experience from our mistakes can help us to effectively learn, yet this way is usually painful and can be very costly. A much better way to learn and mature is to have God reveal to us in His Word what we need to change. This is less agonizing and helps us to trust Jesus even more. Heeding scriptural guidance enables us to avoid many of life's pitfalls.

Every verse has been breathed into life from a loving Heavenly Father, who loves us with an everlasting love! May we commit to intentionally spending time reading Scripture and allow Jesus to speak to us through it daily. Let us then determine to follow what the Bible says over our feelings, desires, emotions, and circumstances.

Day 126 Joy Within

...the joy of the Lord is your strength.

Nehemiah 8:10

Maintaining joy is vital to our survival as Christians. Nehemiah declared our true strength comes from the joy of the Lord. We can instantly add to our joy and the joy of those around us by simply speaking encouraging and positive words.

It should be no surprise to us that Satan works tirelessly to diminish our joy. Stop him in his tracks! Do not allow him to do this! Resist the enemy with powerful words of faith, emitting joy into the environment we are in. Jesus came to earth bringing glad tidings of great joy, overcoming evil with good. He desires for us to be as dedicated as He is to discovering and increasing the good in all things.

We should make every effort to be a blessing to ourselves and others by declaring the promises of God over our lives! May Jesus help us to focus on our blessings and all the good things in life, so we may choose to live joyfully and bring joy to those around us. Joy is the unmistakable sign of God's presence in our lives...for "in thy presence is fulness of joy" (Psalm 16:11). To obtain the full benefits of joy, we must have someone to share it with.

Day 127 God Wants Us to Prosper

Beloved, I wish above all things that you may prosper and be in health, even as your soul prospers.

III John 1:2

Jesus cares about every aspect of our lives. He not only wants Christians to prosper spiritually, but also to prosper physically. True prosperity is so much more than having material possessions and money. When our bodies prosper, we are resilient and physically healthy. Even if we currently have a physical illness, we can pray and expect God to heal us. True prosperity consists also of having peace of mind and contentment.

When our souls prosper, we thrive internally as well. We experience peace. We are filled with joy. We have a sense of purpose. We grow spiritually, and we have healthy and loving relationships with others. Jesus came to give us full and abundant living (see John 10:10). He is the God of all abundance, and He desires for us to live prosperously, filled with thanksgiving, joy, and provision.

May Jesus help us to prosper in body and soul and give us good health and peace as He promised in His Word. Whatever our need is today, whether it is something spiritual, physical, or anything else, we should take the time to praise Him in advance for making us whole!

Day 128 Praying in the Spirit

Praying always with all prayer and supplication in the Spirit, and watching thereunto with all perseverance and supplication for all saints.

Ephesians 6:18

As Christians, we need to have a clear view of who our true enemy is in our ongoing spiritual warfare. In Ephesians 6:12, Apostle Paul informs us that our warfare is "...against principalities, against powers, against the rulers of the darkness of this world, against spiritual wickedness in high places." Praying in the Spirit allows us to fight the enemy on a supernatural level for the benefit of the entire Church, not just ourselves.

We may not realize the type of battle or the particular armor needed at the time; however, powerful outcomes transpire when we pray in the Spirit. We should not procrastinate about prayer, simply waiting for an opportune time to pray. We should pray daily, even when we do not feel like praying. Praying in the Spirit is an invaluable and sacred privilege that enables us to commune with God.

Let us praise Jesus for the honor and privilege He has provided us to go beyond the veil and to worship in the throne room of His loving Presence. Let us commune with Him today in the holy of holies through prayer. May Jesus teach us once again how to pray, not only for ourselves but also for everyone needing His divine help.

Day 129 Stay Alert to Satan's Tricks

Lest Satan should get an advantage of us: for we are not ignorant of his devices.

2 Corinthians 2:11

Today's verse cautions us to understand the enemy's deceptions and snares and to be alert of how he uses his arsenal to attack each of us. When battles, trials, and sufferings come our way, we can choose to give all our worries, doubts, and distresses to Jesus.

No matter how dark the night or how evil the situation, we should remind ourselves that our Heavenly Father is not only near to us in the circumstances, but He also loves us and will provide for us through them. Our task is to be vigilant during the challenging periods. We can easily rejoice in God's love and blessings when everything is going good. Yet, during the dark and gloomy times, we should realize that Satan constantly lurks in the shadows trying to destroy us.

Sometimes we wonder why we experience so many hardships and problems. It could be that Satan has singled us out because of God's divine plan for our lives. The greater our level of faithfulness to Jesus, the more we need to resist Satan and his lies. As we hunger after more of Jesus and continually seek Him with our whole heart, we establish our hearts and minds to obey His Word and to do His will. We will always be victorious in the end!

Day 130 Watch and Pray

Watch and pray, that you enter not into temptation: the spirit indeed is willing, but the flesh is weak.

Matthew 26:41

Prayer is associated with watchfulness. It is usually neglected whenever we fail to watch or do not stay alert. If we remain aware of what is really going on around us and in our world, we readily sense the urgency to pray.

Jesus instructed James, John, and Peter at Gethsemane to watch and pray lest they enter into temptation. Prayer is motivated by compassion and concern. Therefore, we should pray for each other, not criticize and condemn one another. God reveals individuals' needs to us so we can be part of the answer, not part of the problem. We cannot fix people, but Jesus can. If we will pray for them, we can observe the Lord working and shaping their lives to become better.

People who are hurt have a tendency to hurt others and become blind to truth. We should pray for the Lord to open their eyes to the truth, so He can truly set them free. They need Jesus, but if they do not call upon Him, we can intercede on their behalf and see the awesome results of power through prayer.

May we have discerning hearts so we can know how to pray and what to pray for regarding others' lives. So, prayer is really about love, love for Jesus and love for others. We pray because we watch. We watch because we care. Our prayer is an act of love.

Day 131 Led by the Holy Spirit

Howbeit when he, the Spirit of truth, is come, he will guide you into all truth …and he will show you things to come.

John 16:13

What a wonderful gift Jesus has given to born again Christians! We have His Spirit dwelling within! Listening to God's voice through spiritual promptings aligned with His Word enables us to live fully in the present and prepare for the future.

This is one major reason why it is imperative that we spend time in deep spiritual intimacy with Jesus on a daily basis. He will reveal things involving our future and the future of those He has entrusted us to care for. Jesus will reveal what we need to know and when we need to know it so we can follow the divine plans He has for us. We must continually grow in our relationship and spiritual intimacy with Him that we may be keenly sensitive to hearing and obeying His voice.

May we have ears that are spiritually attuned to hear, eyes that are open to spiritual truths, and hearts that are yielded to His leadership, correction, and instruction. Let us determine not to allow obstacles along our journey toward eternity to shake our confidence in God's promises. The Holy Spirit is God's seal that we will make it.

Day 132 True Ministry

Keep yourselves in the love of God…

Jude 1:21

If we genuinely love God, we will love others. When we truly love and care about people, we will encourage them by making them feel valued and respected.

Most individuals have not even began to realize the value that Jesus has for them. We are called His "peculiar treasure." Yet, Satan goes about endlessly working toward causing us and others to feel devalued and insignificant. This is one major reason that Jesus wants us to edify (build up) ourselves and one another in our "most holy faith, praying in the Holy Ghost" (Jude 1:20).

Giving someone a nice compliment does not cost us a thing! Effortless acts of being truthful, kind, and encouraging, brings a smile to our Heavenly Father. True ministry does not need to be an official position, but rather a lifestyle dedicated to inviting sinners to Jesus Christ and encouraging believers in their faith.

Today, we should maintain a positive mindset and make it a ceaseless practice to be friendly with everyone and to sincerely compliment each person we meet. Let us decide to become assertive encouragers, making people feel valued, loved and respected.

Day 133 Defeat Anger Before It Defeats Us

Be angry, and sin not: let not the sun go down upon your wrath: Neither give place to the devil.

Ephesians 4:26-27

Never go to bed angry. If we do, we surrender territory in our soul to Satan, causing anger to fester, and eventually allowing bitterness to take root and to form in our hearts. When the devil gets a grip in our hearts, then he attempts to construct an internal stronghold from which he can conquer additional territory in our soul. Continual forgiveness is a standard we must live by daily. This is the only way we can truly live victoriously.

Jesus promises if we will forgive those who offend us, then He will also forgive our offenses. The tradeoff should be a clear no brainer! Jesus will help us to mature in wisdom and stature through His Spirit and to not be controlled by emotional reactions any longer. We should pray for God to empower us to conquer any anger or bitterness in our hearts immediately.

We must defeat anger or it will defeat us. We cannot carry our anger into Heaven. May we choose to defuse our anger through forgiveness, let go of whatever is eating at us, and move forward in the destiny God has in store.

Day 134 Words from the Heart

Out of the abundance of the heart the mouth speaks.

Luke 6:45

Our mouth speaks what our heart is full of. When we are unhappy and disappointed with ourselves, we can easily become critical of others. Jesus said that a tree is known by its fruit. It all begins with a thought. If we allow negative and unkind thoughts to fill our minds, they bear fruit. If we dwell on the bad, we produce bad fruit. We may try to change our words without changing our thoughts; however, we should start with changing the inside first.

Kind or judgmental words do not simply come to us; they come out of our mouths because we have nurtured them in our minds. The more we open ourselves to the Holy Spirit and embrace a Christlike mindset, the more we pray and desire to read our Bible. This results in producing good fruit on the inside and that good fruit shows itself by the way we behave toward others. Sometimes we do a good job of controlling our tongues in public, but when we are at home or when we are around those with whom we are closest we reveal our true character.

Today, we should ask Jesus to forgive us for any negative thoughts we have allowed to fill our minds regarding ourselves and others. Focus on healthy and positive thoughts and on loving and caring for others like Jesus does for us. May Jesus purify our hearts so that our lips speak words of praise to His name and edification to our loved ones and others in our lives.

Day 135 Stop Worrying and Start Praying

Be careful for nothing; but in everything by prayer and supplication with thanksgiving let your requests be made known unto God.

Philippians 4:6

The phrase "be careful for nothing" means literally "don't worry about a single thing." We can become "sick with worry." Think about everything we have worried about in our lives and how eventually it all worked out.

Worry is forbidden in Scripture for believers. It is a sure sign of unbelief; and the Bible labels unbelief and worry as sin. How can we stop worrying? Not in our own willpower, "but in everything by prayer and supplication with thanksgiving let your requests be made known unto God." Pray first in every situation, regardless of how big or small, and express praise and thanksgiving to Jesus in advance. We make our request to Him and experience peace. The peace of God that surpasses all understanding will keep our hearts and minds in Christ Jesus.

We should stop worrying and quit complicating our life by trying to figure out everything in advance. May we trust Jesus enough to do what He has asked us to do daily. Then we can enjoy living, and He will provide solutions and answers to our questions and problems in due time. May He grant us supernatural peace in Jesus name.

Day 136 Thirsting for Jesus

O God, you are my God; early will I seek you: my soul thirsts for you, my flesh longs for you in a dry and thirsty land, where no water is.

Psalm 63:1

Intimacy with God requires time. Not everyone is willing to take the required time to be close to Jesus. We often tell ourselves we do not have time to seek God. However, we always seem to have the time to do things that are most important to us. Although our lives may be filled with distractions, when talking to and knowing Jesus becomes significant enough, we will find the time for Him.

We should stop trying to fit Jesus into our schedule, but instead work our schedules around time spent with Him. When we neglect time with the Lord, the complications and problems in our daily life entangle us and we no longer have the perspective we need to see our way through. When we spend time with the Lord, we discover that we become better at making decisions and better at seeing the heart of whatever issue we are facing. We are then able to adapt our lives appropriately.

We should seek after Jesus like a person stranded in the desert seeks for water! We should long for Him and anxiously anticipate spending time in His presence. A few minutes with Jesus in intimate prayer each day refreshes us more than a vacation and equips us to handle any situation. Starting today, let us make our devotional time the foundation of our days, for we cannot possibly survive without spending time with Jesus.

Day 137 Turning Mistakes Into Miracles

A new heart also will I give you, and a new spirit will I put within you…

Exodus 36:26

Jesus will turn our mistakes into miracles if we will let Him. Joseph's brothers, having evil intentions, sold him into slavery. Elderly Sarah impatiently asked her husband, Abraham, to have a child with Hagar. King David had an adulterous affair with Bathsheba. In each of these examples, God forgave their sinful acts and did wonders for them. Joseph became the second in command of the Egyptian Empire, where he rescued his brothers and his entire family from starvation. Sarah had a miracle child by Abraham and even Hagar's son, Ishmael, was the beginning of a great nation. After the death of their first child, Bathsheba bore for David the next king of Israel, Solomon, who became the wisest leader in history, other than Christ Himself.

Jesus specializes in turning our mistakes into miracles! Each of us probably have struggled with powerful strongholds, addictions, or suffered some type of abuse, by which we wondered if we would survive or even have a life worth living. God met us where we were, embraced, loved, and healed us. When we give Jesus our mistakes, He removes the shame, scars, and pain and shapes them into something wonderful and beautiful in our lives, and empowers us to draw from these experiences to rescue others.

We all make mistakes and certainly regret things from our past. However, we are not our mistakes, and we are here now with God's power to shape our day and our future.

Day 138 Loving Unlikeable People

Hatred stirs up strife: but love covers all sins.

Proverbs 10:12

Zig Ziglar said, "Never blame anyone in your life. Good people give you happiness. Bad people give you experience. Worst people give you a lesson. And best people give you memories." Sometimes we must deal with people we do not like. It may be their personality, demeanor, or something about them that just does not sit well with us. In order to refrain from becoming negative about others or our time with them, we should see people the way Jesus sees them, which is to view each person as a possibility rather than a problem.

Loving like Jesus starts in the mind. The way we think, positively or negatively, greatly affects us and the people around us. Where our mind directs, our words and actions follow (see Proverbs 23:7). We may not like everyone we meet, yet we are expected to love them. Those we avoid may be hurting inside and possibly need us the most to witness to them or to be a light of hope in God for them. Remember that there is more to the person's story than we may realize. Stop judging them and simply love them.

"You are the light of the world" (Matthew 5:14). When we love people in spite of their faults, we experience the love of Jesus for us in spite of our flaws. Let us stay positive, believe for the best in others, and love like Jesus loves.

Day 139 Great Peace

Great peace have they which love your law and nothing shall offend them.

Psalm 119:165

The word "offend" in this case means "to cause to stumble." When we walk in peace, we do not stumble through life continually making bad choices or mistakes. Jesus gives or takes peace from our conscience to let us know whether or not we are on the right path. For us to discern the voice of God from other voices vying for our attention, we should heed the voice that brings the peace of God into our hearts.

Possessing peace contributes to preserving power in our lives. Lack of peace is usually a signal that we are making a mistake or are about to make one. Do not act until there is peace. Internal peace confirms for us that Jesus approves of our direction. Since the peace of God rules on the inside, we no longer have to be a victim with wounded emotions. The peace of Jesus keeps our lives from being ruled by treatment from others, "nothing shall offend!"

Today, we should praise and thank Jesus for leading and guiding us into His perfect will. May He help us to become more sensitive to His Holy Spirit and follow His peace in every decision. Peace with God gives us the "great peace" of God.

Day 140 Good Friends

Iron sharpens iron; so a man sharpens the countenance of his friend.

Proverbs 27:17

A common phrase is "a person is known by the company he or she keeps." We love having friends and Jesus wants us to have them. However, His Word emphasizes that these should be healthy, safe, and godly relationships.

Relationships may be harmful for us when we are being manipulated and taken advantage of. We should value ourselves enough to confront unhealthy relationships, speaking the truth in love (see Ephesians 4:15). We are valuable to God and are permitted to have wholesome friends who will respect and honor us appropriately.

Not only do we want to avoid bad friendships, but we also need to form good and wholesome friendships. If someone wants to become better at cooking, playing a sport, working a trade, or practically anything, the best thing this person can do is make friends with someone who is really good at it. If we desire to be a better Christian, then choose friends who love Jesus sincerely with all their hearts. Seek out friends who motivate us to do better.

Let us put our energy into finding good friends. May Jesus help us to always be a good friend and may He give us safe, healthy relationships in which we can flourish and grow.

Day 141 Our Great God Within

You are of God, little children, and have overcome them: because greater is he that is in you, than he that is in the world.

I John 4:4

We were created by Jesus to do great things. But without genuine confidence we cannot realize our destiny. We are not to be confident in ourselves but in Christ Jesus dwelling within.

Satan attempts to minimize our confidence through fear and intimidation; however, we have calm assurance that GREATER is Christ within us! Jesus is able even if were are not. He is waiting and watching for us to demonstrate confidence in Him. Faith opens God's greatness to be seen through our lives, so we should trust Him and rejoice in the peace and power of a confident life.

We should proclaim these promises in our hearts and souls until confident faith arises within. "I can do all things through Christ which strengthens me" (Philippians 4:13) and "…With God all things are possible" (Mark 10:27). To be overcoming and victorious, we must realize our true identity. We triumph through the unstoppable power of Christ Jesus and His unfailing love. Our God, who is greater, has birthed His greatness in us! Greater is Christ within us than he who is in the world!

Day 142 Jesus will Carry Us

Come unto me, all you that labor and are heavy laden, and I will give you rest. Take my yoke upon you, and learn of me; for I am meek and lowly in heart: and you shall find rest unto your souls.

Matthew 11:28-29

Learning to let our souls rest is essential to our wellbeing. This scriptural passage indicates refreshment, renewal and holy serenity for our souls. Jesus offers us rest, a vacation for our souls, an escape for our inner lives.

When we are overloaded, tired, and drained from the weight of the world, we can spend time with Jesus and attain His promise to give us rest in His presence. He will carry us when we cannot carry on. Our Christian walk is not about doing our best and allowing Jesus to do the rest. It is about completely surrendering to God and giving Him control over our lives and letting Him carry our burdens.

Let us give God all our pressures, anxieties, and cares, allowing Him to refresh our spirits and souls. May we give our all to Jesus today. He will care for us much better than we could ever care for ourselves.

Day 143 Promotion from the Lord

For promotion cometh neither from the east, nor from the west, nor from the south. But God is the judge: he puts down one, and sets up another.

Psalm 75:6-7

Promotion comes from God the Righteous Judge. The psalmist explains this clearly and simply so that there can be no mistake: God exalts one and humbles another. He is in control.

We often try to rely on our human ability in dealing with opposition and adversity or to gain support and attain promotion. Today's scriptural passage informs us that achievement and success is from the Lord. No demon from hell can hinder or stop us when God is ready to move in our lives. Regardless of what others think of us, our God shows Himself strong through our weaknesses and inabilities. His reasons are not based on our talents or capabilities, but on a heart that is willing and surrendered to Him. Jesus focuses on our availability over our ability.

When we show that we are truly dedicated in the small things He has blessed us with, we will be given the opportunity to rise to the next level. May we be diligent now so that we are well equipped with the right attitude to do well with what we will be given in the future. Jesus will establish us, our reputation, career, and future. He may not move when we want Him to, but He is always on time. At just the right moment, He will deliver us from adversity and help us to realize our goals.

Day 144 No Fear, Trust and Believe

For God has not given us the spirit of fear; but of power, and of love, and of a sound mind.

2 Timothy 1:7

Our world is rampant with insecurity and people lacking confidence. We cannot function in both courage and fear at the same time. Like oil and water, they just don't mix well together. We may experience some fear, but we must not allow it to control us. Instead, we should trust securely in the love of Jesus, that He will work all things together for our good (see Romans 8:28).

We should trust God and step out in faith to do whatever He asks us to do and do not withdraw in fear and silence. We ought to walk each day with the realization that God's angels are going before and behind us. Jesus is with us and nothing can defeat us. We should not be afraid of uncertainty or the unknown because we serve a God who knows all.

Never fear the challenges facing us, for our Lord will empower and strengthen us to accomplish much more than we thought possible. May Jesus liberate us from fear and worry and cause us to be confident and courageous. Keep trusting and believing. All things are possible to those who believe.

Day 145 Finish Strong

But none of these things move me, neither count I my life dear unto myself, so that I might finish my course with joy…

Acts 20:24

Paul's mind was not on the sufferings he had endured or those which were to follow. His heart and soul were on completing God's purpose for him. It is not how we begin the race, it is how we finish it.

We need to always finish well with everything we attempt to do. We never feel good about ourselves when we quit anything or never finish what we started. We should stand strong in faith, realizing that Jesus is with us and that He wants us to finish our race well. Even when we are exhausted and feel like quitting, we should remember the joy we will experience by completing our divine course. It requires determination to finish our race with joy!

The power and grace of Jesus will enable us to press onward through every difficulty. Today, let us recommit to doing the work before us and to finishing what we have started, no matter how great the challenge. May we allow Jesus to be our strength as we press onward toward the prize and finish our race strong.

Day 146 Necessary Suffering

For unto you it is given in the behalf of Christ, not only to believe on him, but also to suffer for his sake.

Philippians 1:29

We have the dual privilege today of believing on Jesus and of suffering on His behalf. If we are not prepared to suffer, we should just forget about being a Christian, for Scripture warns us that all who live godly in Christ Jesus shall suffer persecution. In the world, Jesus said, "You shall have tribulation, but be of good cheer, I have overcome the world."

God wisely shaped life to include suffering. It is not a sacrifice, but a privilege that He has given us, to suffer for His name. Suffering is necessary for our Christian development. However, we need not fear during the struggle. Fear is from Satan and can separate us from faith in God. It is impossible to avoid all suffering. Sometimes we try to build emotional walls in order not to be hurt. When we build walls to shut others out, we can also shut ourselves in. We can by faith break down the wall of fear, give Jesus our scars and rely on His grace for healing. Take any new hurts immediately to Him, refusing to let them fester. "For I will restore health unto you, and I will heal you of your wounds, says the Lord" (Jeremiah 30:17).

Jesus has created us to share His truth and love with others. May Jesus enable us to reach out in freedom and heal any wounds that may be preventing us from loving people the way He loves them. Joy is not the absence of suffering, but rather it entertains the Presence of God.

Day 147 Maintain a Delightful Attitude

Delight yourself also in the Lord: and he shall give you the desires of your heart.

Psalm 37:4

God has put desires within our hearts to achieve and succeed…and this is good. He also promises He will fulfill our desires as we draw closer to Him, neither will He withhold any good thing from us, if we do what is right (see Psalm 84:11).

We cannot enjoy the present and the blessings it contains if we do not have the right attitude toward work. Mary and Martha were two sisters with contrasting attitudes (see Luke 10: 38–42). Martha was overly engaged and very busy, but Mary sat at the feet of Jesus and listened intently to what He was saying. Jesus said Mary made the better choice in listening and soaking it all in. He did not tell Martha not to work, yet He did suggest that she not be irritated or have a bad attitude while working. Jesus wants us to work and give our best effort, but He also wants us to be wise enough to realize when we should stop all activity in order not to let the timely miracle slip past us without us noticing it or receiving it.

Fall in love with Jesus. Take time every day to sit quietly in His presence. Learn to delight in Him. May God help us to stay balanced and not miss our "timely miracle."

Day 148 Trust in Jesus and Do Good

Trust in the Lord, and do good; so shall you dwell in the land, and verily you shall be fed.

Psalm 37:3

We often become distracted in the midst of difficulties and adversities and waste valuable time and resources on them. We simply should stay focused on our purpose, do good and keep commitments we have made. Anytime we dwell on God's faithfulness and let it encourage our hearts and souls, our faith increases and matures.

As we focus on doing good, our thoughts remain positive. Rather than allowing our thoughts to dwell on past discouragement or hardships, we can place our trust in Jesus and live in peace with joy and love. If we will continue our study of God's Word, keep praying, maintain commitments, and persist in helping others, our breakthrough happens more quickly. Reaching out and being a blessing to others while we are hurting is truly powerful.

Having assurance of God's provision is dependent on two primary principles—trusting in Him and doing good to others. By doing this, we learn to trust the Lord in new ways that bring renewed hope and joy. May Jesus help us to function independently of our problems and to respond by helping and blessing others. With His grace and strength, we can continue doing good and being a positive influence.

Day 149 A Good Attitude

Do all things without murmurings and disputes.

Philippians 2:14

If we decide ahead of time that we will not be happy or at peace unless we get exactly what we want, then we will seldom experience peace and fulfillment. When we think like this, we prepare ourselves to be unhappy and to lose our contentment before we even have a problem. Instead of expecting to be upset, we can choose to be at peace.

Our joy comes from our relationship with Jesus. So we should determine to be happy and to have rest in our souls regardless of what looming difficulties we must deal with. Whether things go well or not, whether people like us or not, we will choose to walk in the joy of the Lord! Our attitude about our lives makes the difference in the quality of life we experience. Even if we cannot fix our problems readily, we can fix the way we think about them.

"Ability is what you're capable of doing. Motivation determines what you do. Attitude determines how well you do it" (Lou Holtz). May Jesus help us to face life with a good attitude, positive and full of faith, and to habitually prepare for the best in every circumstance.

Day 150 Valley of Decision

Multitudes, multitudes in the valley of decision: for the day of the Lord is near in the valley of decision.

Joel 3:14

In moments of decisions our destiny is shaped. During emotional peaks and chaotic environments, people can easily make extremely bad decisions that negatively impact their lives for years. In such cases, we should wait until the dust adequately settles, when we are thinking rationally and we are calm before deciding what and how to move, or whether we should simply do nothing.

After we have prayed earnestly about a situation and have considered all available options, it is time to trust God. The toughest part after making a difficult decision can be trusting God with it. If we make our decision based on prayer, scriptural principle, and seeking wise godly counsel, we can take comfort in knowing that we have obeyed the Lord in making the right decision.

Let us make good and godly decisions today so we can walk in the destiny God has planned for us. May Jesus help us not to feel pressured into making decisions before knowing His will. May He also empower us to make informed and wise choices that align with His divine plan for our lives.

Day 151 Do All Things with Excellence

Whatsoever your hand finds to do, do it with your might.

Ecclesiastes 9:10

Pursuing excellence means striving to do the best we can with the gifts, talents, and abilities God has provided us and giving our best effort for His glory. It begins with developing excellent habits in little things, which prepares us to achieve excellence in greater things.

We should strive to be better today than we were yesterday and even better tomorrow than we are today. We can do great and mighty things through Christ who strengthens and empowers us to rise above mediocrity and promote excellence not only in ourselves, but also in the lives of those we touch. We ought to work with delight and determination. Diligence gives us favor. "See a man diligent in his business? he shall stand before kings…" (Proverbs 22:29). This is wonderful motivation for us to do all things with excellence.

Let us determine to do the task Jesus provides us this day heartily as unto Him. May we despise mediocrity in ourselves and cast off complacency. May we rather embrace a life of excellence in everything for His glory.

Day 152 Tough Love

Now no chastening for the present seems to be joyous, but grievous: nevertheless afterward it yields the peaceable fruit of righteousness unto them which are exercised thereby.

Hebrews 12:11

Sometimes we should apply tough love to ourselves and others. Instead of simply feeling sorry for people, Jesus often provokes them to action. He struck Paul with blindness for a short period so Paul could clearly see (Acts 9). Paul then went to Ananias. After Ananias prayed for Paul, Paul received the infilling of the Holy Ghost and his sight was restored. Paul became empowered to preach Jesus and to spread the gospel everywhere. He even wrote half the New Testament books!

We may be going through a tough time right now. But what great things does God have planned for us? Jesus could be desiring for us to get our minds off ourselves and our problems. He might be motivating us to do something about them. We sometimes feel we are being mean if we confront people, when in reality tough love is what God often used to set people free.

May Jesus help us to love people enough to speak the truth and grant us wisdom to know when and how to apply tough love so they can experience greater freedom too. May we also be thankful for the tough love that Jesus shows us, that He is willing to do whatever is needed to bring about positive change in our lives, and let us we be thankful He is persistent.

Day 153 God's Masterpiece

All scripture is given by inspiration of God, and is profitable for doctrine, for reproof, for correction, for instruction in righteousness: That the man of God may be perfect, thoroughly furnished unto all good works.

2 Timothy 3:16-17

Jesus has provided us everything we need to complete our divine purpose through His Word. Visualize the Holy Spirit positioned in front of us as clay or unchiseled stone. As we read, study, and meditate on Scripture, the Spirit uses each verse to mold and shape us into the remarkable individuals we are meant to become. The masterpiece is still us, just as clay molded by a potter is the same clay or chiseled stone is the same marble. As the Spirit of God chisels or molds away at us with the Truths of Scripture, we become more each day like Jesus. The Spirit of God uses Scripture to fashion us for the blessed life that He has in store for us.

We have the ideas, the creativity and talent to successfully complete our mission. God's anointing empowers us to do what we could not do on our own, to accomplish goals and aspirations, even if we do not possess the natural talent, and to overcome difficulties that seem impossible. Jesus has equipped us and is working on our behalf. He is aligning the right people to meet us and preparing opportunities for our future. We have all we need to live a victorious life.

May Jesus Help us to remain focused on His Word and His plan. May He use His Word to make us useful as His Spirit molds and shapes us into people with purpose!

Day 154 Put On a New Garment

To appoint unto them that mourn in Zion, to give unto them … the garment of praise for the spirit of heaviness; that they might be called trees of righteousness, the planting of the Lord…

Isaiah 61:3

Somedays we do not find it easy to feel grateful or joyful. Satanic and worldly oppression attempts endlessly to place the spirit of heaviness upon us. On days like this, we must offer up to Jesus the sacrifice of praise and put on a new garment of praise for our hearts and minds. Anytime we feel the enemy attempting to place heavy-heartedness or discouragement on us, we must replace it with praise and thanksgiving unto our God. Offering unto Him sacrifices of praise drives away the spirit of heaviness.

Jesus knows life is not always simple or easy for us. Sometimes we may feel weary and gloomy, yet we realize He is always wonderful and good. Therefore we will put on new garments and give God praise! We praise Him for restoration and blessing in advance! Whenever we do this, we will "be called trees of righteousness, the planting of the Lord, that he might be glorified."

The spirit of heaviness has no place in us anymore because God's Spirit is working within to make us complete in Him. Our mourning is turned to joy. We trade our heaviness for garments of praise. Praise Him for securing us in Him and His righteousness, like a tree planted in good ground where it can flourish. Jesus, please make us new today!

Day 155 From Ordinary to Extraordinary

Therefore if any man be in Christ, he is a new creature: old things are passed away; behold, all things are become new.

2 Corinthians 5:17

We all appreciate "do-overs" or second chances. Jesus does much better than that! He enables us to become new again. When we receive Jesus Christ as our Savior and are filled with His Spirit, we trade our old life for a new one. We trade sin for forgiveness, pride for humility, legalism for grace, fear for love, weakness for strength, and sadness for joy.

When the Holy Spirit lives within, the Lord begins to remove layers of deceit and doubt that obscure our vision of Him which hinder us from mirroring His image in our lives. Jesus daily removes old thoughts and habits that bind us and replaces them with His loving truth. Although reverberations of our previous life will try to return, Christ within empowers us to overcome them. At times, we may feel we have not changed. However, we can be confident in knowing, if we are living in obedience to Scripture, we are far from the old person we once were! If we stay sensitive to what the Holy Spirit desires, we will make godly choices.

Let us praise God for making us fresh and new! We are free from sin and death! Each of us are ordinary people who have been made extraordinary by the Spirit within.

Day 156 Destined to Soar

...They shall mount up with wings as eagles...

Isaiah 40:31

Like eagles, WE WERE DESTINED TO SOAR! This is why we experience discomfort and frustration when simply trying to exist in mediocrity or in the mundane. Jesus has a magnificent purpose for our lives. This is why we sense an intrinsic yearning to excel and reach for the stars.

Sometimes friends around us do not understand this and may try to "clip our wings" with unsupportive or discouraging words. They may even cause us to question ourselves and our motives by making us think, "Why can't we just be normal?" The reason is, we can never be satisfied with "normal" when God has birthed in us a destiny to soar!

We are meant to soar like eagles! Reach for greatness! Never stop dreaming! May Jesus nurture this inner desire within us to ascend for greatness. Let us be confident and never settle for anything less than our best. We are not just any ole bird! We were made to fly! We are destined to soar!

Day 157 Right Attitude No Matter What

But as for you, you thought evil against me; but God meant it unto good, to bring to pass, as it is this day, to save much people alive.

Genesis 50:20

Joseph was a visionary who realized God wanted to accomplish greatness through his life. He was betrayed and sold into slavery by his brothers, falsely accused by Potiphar's wife, throne into prison, and forgotten by the butler who promised to help him. Each time rather than becoming bitter, he became better. Because he chose the right attitude, God elevated Joseph from prison to the palace of the Egyptian empire, where he rescued his family from certain extinction.

We have one of two options on how we choose to respond to bad things happening in our lives, we can either become bitter or choose to become better. Regardless of what someone may have done to us, Jesus provides us the power to forgive them. He can give us peace and contentment even in difficult situations. However, we must ask Jesus to help us love those we dislike, regardless of how they act toward us. Forgiving and loving people does not mean we become their punching bag. It does mean that we begin to see them as God sees them. No one can rob us of our joy if we place our complete trust in Jesus Christ.

Let us choose the right attitude and look beyond the present in realizing the higher purpose and calling Jesus has in store for us. May Jesus empower us to have love for others regardless of how they may treat us. Today, we determine to always become better and never bitter!

Day 158 What Do We Want?

What things so ever you desire, when you pray, believe that you receive them, and you shall have them.

Mark 11:24

By this verse, it appears as though all we have to do is ask God for anything and we can have it. Yet, that is not completely true. The truth is, prayer is not about bringing our wish list to Jesus and waiting for Him to send our gifts. Prayer is about coming humbly before the Lord and receiving whatever good gift He prefers to offer us.

We must first sincerely seek His kingdom and righteousness (see Matthew 6:33). As we spend time in the presence of Jesus, our thoughts and desires become better aligned with His purpose. We then prepare ourselves to ask Him for anything. He subsequently will give it to us since we want what He wants.

Jesus expects us to ask boldly in faith. However, sometimes we are hesitant to ask Him for big things. Indecisiveness and reluctance can become barriers in our minds, causing confusion, insecurity, and rendering us ineffective. God desires that we conquer doubt by trusting, believing and then receiving the answer to our prayers from Him.

Prayer is more about drawing closer to Jesus than getting what we ask for. May Jesus help us to overcome doubtful predispositions that prevent us from moving forward in His divine purpose for us and to always want what He wants.

Day 159 Build a Scriptural Fortress

For as he thinks in his heart, so is he.

Proverbs 23:7

Our inward thoughts, words, and even words spoken to ourselves matter. They can dictate the course of our lives and our decisions. This is why it is vital to make sure that our thoughts are grounded in scriptural truth. We should determine to set our hearts and minds on what we desire to occur during our day, rather than submissively waiting for whatever thoughts and events might happen.

As basic as we choose what to wear, we can be selective in our thinking and how we will respond to things, especially since what we dwell on typically turns into reality for us. Therefore, let us choose to think positive thoughts and focus our hearts and minds on being strong, energetic, and content. If we fill our hearts and minds with the right things, the wrong things will not have any room to enter. God's Word provides protection over our hearts and lives, in which we can build a scriptural fortress in our minds so not just any old thought can come in. We can place our expectation in the Lord, who is waiting and willing to bless us.

Confident expectancy activates faith into reality! May God forgive our lack of faith and our passive thoughts, and help us to focus our minds in a way that will release Him to do His best in us. Let us liberate our faith today to believe Jesus will accomplish His best in our lives.

Day 160 Correction Is Evidence of God's Love

I will praise you; for I am fearfully and wonderfully made: marvelous are your works; and that my soul knows right well.

Psalm 139:14

Regardless of our flaws, we can accept and embrace ourselves as God's unique creation. God can change us. The change process, however, cannot start until self-acceptance is resolved in our lives individually.

Self-acceptance begins with believing that Jesus loves us unconditionally, just as we are. Once we have established this in our hearts, we will experience a deeper intimacy in Him and become willing to accept His correction, which is needed for real change to occur. Individuals who do not realize they are loved have difficulty in receiving correction. Correction is basically Jesus giving us divine direction for our lives, guiding us to better things. However, if we are insecure, we will constantly feel condemned by correction instead of joyfully embracing it as an opportunity to improve.

May we be patient with ourselves and allow the Lord to shape us for our best life. Today, we should thank God for His unconditional love and acceptance. May Jesus help us to always accept His correction as an indication of His unfailing love and care for us.

Day 161 Be Kind to Self

And as you would that men should do to you, do you also to them likewise.

Luke 6:31

The way we treat ourselves is usually the way we will treat others in our lives. If we accept the mercy of Jesus, then we will show mercy to others. However, if we are unhappy, unsatisfied and hard on ourselves, we will behave toward others similarly. If we cannot love ourselves, we will not be able to love others.

If we are incompassionate toward ourselves, then we will be incapable of genuine compassion for others. We should respect, value, and be good to ourselves without being self-centered or arrogant. We need to view ourselves honestly, knowing what our strengths and weaknesses are, yet realizing our Lord's grace is sufficient for us and His strength is perfected in our weaknesses (see 2 Corinthians 12:9). We should stop being distressed over our deficiencies and imperfections. Everyone has faults. This is why we need Jesus!

May Jesus help us to maintain realistic expectations of ourselves and others, understanding everyone has weaknesses, and we all need His love, power, strength and support each day. May we also learn to love and forgive ourselves. When we have the right attitude toward ourselves, we will have the right attitude toward others.

Day 162 Guarded by Angels

For he shall give his angels charge over you, to keep you in all your ways. They shall bear you up in their hands, lest you dash your foot against a stone.

Psalm 91:11-12

Sometimes our days get off to a bad start and it seems we simply can never catch up. If someone upsets us at the beginning of the morning, we may have a short fuse and become defensive the entire day. Or, even if our day begins in a rush, we seem to rush the rest of the day and cannot manage to slow things down. We should start our days with a positive attitude focused on Scripture, determined not to have a bad day.

Regardless of how difficult things may be today, we can take comfort in knowing that Jesus is always with us. God's angels will help to keep our path safe and secure. They will "bear us up in their hands," even if we stub a toe (see Psalm 91:11-12). If He cares enough to protect us in minor difficulties, imagine how He will guard us in all other areas of our lives.

May Jesus help us to begin our day on the right path and in the right pace and help us to have a positive mindset focused on Him. He will take care of us! He will take care of the problems. Trust Him!

Day 163 Blessed to Be a Blessing

I will bless the Lord at all times: his praise shall continually be in my mouth.

Psalm 34:1

This day provides the wonderful opportunity to express our gratitude to Jesus. Irrespective of how problematic this time in our lives has been, we can raise holy hands in praise to Him for all the great things He has done!

As we bless the Lord, He blesses and empowers us to be a blessing to others. Everyone could use a blessing. Each person needs love, encouragement, edification, compliments, and appreciation. Everyone desires to feel valued and cared for. Jesus blesses us so we can be a blessing.

Let us magnify and exalt the Most High God for all the blessings in our lives and for empowering us to be a blessing to others. May Jesus help us to reach out and bless others daily in bringing encouragement to their lives.

Day 164 Test Everything with Scripture

Prove all things; hold fast that which is good.

I Thessalonians 5:21

Hearing from God clearly and avoiding deception stems solely from spending habitual time with Him and studying His Word. Knowing the Bible protects us from deception.

Individuals who attempt to be led by the Spirit, but are too lazy to spend time in the Word and prayer, easily fall into deception by evil spirits or dishonest people. When Satan tried to tempt and deceive Jesus, His reply was "It is written…" and then He quoted Scripture to reject Satan's lies (see Luke 4). The Apostle Paul told us to test all things, yet we have accepted words and counsel without testing them in the past. Rather than rejecting everything told to us as "thus saith the Lord," because some were misleading, we need to take responsibility to prove what is spoken to us. We should welcome everything the Holy Spirit speaks.

May Jesus help us to learn how to recognize what is real and what is counterfeit. We need to validate everything we hear by the Word of God, because it is the only accurate measure of truth that exists. May God help us to hear His voice clearly and to always test everything we believe by the perfect standard of His Word.

Day 165 Prayer, Our First Response

Hitherto have you asked nothing in my name: ask, and you shall receive, that your joy may be full.

John 16:24

We frequently spend much of our time complaining about our problems and trying to figure out how to solve them on our own. If we do not pray, Jesus may choose to do nothing, even though He is ever present with us. Prayer is our license for God's intervention.

We often do everything except the one thing Jesus told us to do…to ask in His name. He wants to provide for our every need. We ask and receive so that our joy may be full. Jesus wants us happy and full of joy. He does not desire for us to be discouraged and hopeless. We have the wonderful privilege of simply "asking and receiving." Therefore, we should always pray as a first response to every situation.

In obedience to scriptural Truth, instead of complaining about what we do not want, let us ask God for what we do want. Then, rejoice and be glad for the promise that whatsoever we ask according to His will in the name of Jesus, He will grant us. Let us praise our God today and thank Him that we can bring all our needs to Him. May we always choose prayer as our first option, knowing that Jesus delights in caring for us.

Day 166 Forgiving Hearts

And when you stand praying, forgive, if ye have aught against any: that your Father also which is in heaven may forgive you your trespasses.

Mark 11:25

One of the most challenging practices in life is forgiving others. Letting go of anger and hurt feelings caused by the wrongdoings of another seems hard. Even if we are justified in our disdain for the individual, nothing good ever comes from harboring negative emotions.

Jesus forgives us of so much more than we will ever need to forgive of others. Realizing this should enable us to readily and easily forgive. We may not have done what others have done to us; but then again, we may do things that are even worse. God does not view sin as being little or big sin…sin is sin. We should do ourselves a favor and forgive quickly and freely without expectations or stipulations. The longer we hold a grudge, the more difficult it is to let it go.

The key to forgiving others is diligence in maintaining our personal relationship with Jesus. This means trusting Him with our lives. When we find it impossible to release our resentment, let us place ourselves in the everlasting arms of our Lord and find the inner-strength to conquer the impossible! May we pray and determine to have a forgiving heart like Jesus.

Day 167 Redeeming Our Time

Walk in wisdom toward them that are without, redeeming the time.

Colossians 4:5

People often set unrealistic goals and constantly fail to achieve them. A little bit of foresight and planning could have saved them from considerable difficulty and irritation. We should be realistic about how long it will take to complete tasks and give ourselves sufficient time to finish them without becoming overly stressed.

It is okay to say no to requests from people who want us to do things for them. We are required to meet God's expectations of us, not necessarily everyone else's. If we will take the necessary time to plan ahead before committing ourselves to things, we will be astonished at how much more time, energy, and peace of mind we will save in the long run.

A life lived for Jesus is an investment of time. It takes time building up our testimony. It takes time sharing with people, being astute to the timing of what we say and looking for those moments when their hearts are ready to receive. This requires patience, because individuals do not necessarily respond as soon as we would like.

Let us make the best use of all time we have been given. May Jesus help us to plan wisely so we can live with joy and do everything He has called us to do and to also apply this wisdom in determining the right commitments.

Day 168 Confidence in Jesus Christ

For the Lord shall be your confidence…

Proverbs 3:26

Our world is filled with individuals who struggle with self-doubt, which causes them to live in fear and to focus mainly on their limitations and flaws and what others think of them. Having Christ within liberates us from self-doubt as we live by faith fully trusting Him.

In Jesus, we are part of a "chosen generation" and a "royal priesthood" (see I Peter 2:9). Quite often the most difficult part of life's journey is believing that we are worth the trip. We should stop looking to people to determine our value. Self-respect, self-worth, and self-love all start with knowing and loving Jesus Christ. Our confidence should not rest in the things of this world, but rather be confident in knowing that the Most High God will protect us and keep us from falling.

Without Jesus watching over us, we are likely to fall for Satan's tricks. If we pray, read and live by God's Word, we will be safe in the presence of our loving and unfailing God. "I am crucified with Christ: nevertheless I live; yet not I, but Christ lives in me: and the life which I now live in the flesh I live by the faith of the Son of God, who loved me, and gave himself for me" (Galatians 2:20).

Day 169 A Fair Trade

...To give unto them beauty for ashes, the oil of joy for mourning, the garment of praise for the spirit of heaviness...

Isaiah 61:3

Jesus wants to make a trade with us today. He asks us to give Him all our worries, troubles, failures and disappointments. In exchange, He will give us His joy and peace. In addition, He pledges to protect and care for us.

When we trust Jesus, we are able to rest in Him realizing that He has the situation well in hand. Conversely, worry steals our peace, exhausts us physically, and can even make us ill. We need to give Jesus our worry and He will give to us His peace in exchange. As we give Him all our cares and fears, He will give us His security, strength and joy. What an ideal trade this is to our advantage! This is the great benefit to being cared for by Jesus. "Casting all your care upon him; for he cares for you" (I Peter 5:7).

Let us put on garments of praise. May we awake to the fulfilled life Jesus has provided us through salvation and live so that others may be drawn to Him.

Day 170 Worship Rather Than Worry

Ah Lord God! behold, you have made the heaven and the earth by your great power and stretched out arm, and there is nothing too hard for you.

Jeremiah 32:17

Are we worried about anything today? We naturally worry during threatening times. Rather than worrying, Jesus wants us to worship.

An effective way to worship Him is to simply believe in who He is and what He is able to do. We should pray and focus on His amazing character and great power. "…For with God all things are possible" (Mark 10:27). Jesus can handle anything, including all that we are currently dealing with. "Behold, the Lord's hand is not shortened, that it cannot save; neither his ear heavy, that it cannot hear" (Isaiah 59:1). He knows each of us personally and by name. Jesus demonstrates His love for us in that, He not only knows us, He cares for us and yearns to bring us closer to Him.

We should remind ourselves of what God has done for us and others. Allow this to build our confidence in trusting that He will help us continually. Rather than worrying, take time to pray, remember who the Most High God is and what He is capable of. Trust that He will help us through any problems we confront. One day we will see Jesus face to face!

Day 171 Obtaining God's Favor

And the child Samuel grew on, and was in favor both with the Lord, and also with men.

I Samuel 2:26

Samuel sought God's favor first. As a result, others found favor with him recognizing his wisdom and connectedness to God. Some individuals only seek the favor of people, which puts them in bondage to having to maintain this level of favor. Rather than seeking others' favor, let us seek the supernatural favor of Jesus.

People will recognize the wisdom and growth resulting from our genuine relationship with the Lord, and then grant us their favor too, bringing glory to God. When we obtain His favor, great things begin to happen in our lives, true joy and abundant blessings! Jesus shines graciousness on us daily. It can be something as simple as finding the perfect parking spot, or reconnecting with an old friend precisely when we needed to. If we look for His blessings, we will find them.

"A good man obtains favor of the Lord…" (Proverbs 12:2). Let us do good today so we may walk in the favor of the Lord!

Day 172 Winning the Battle of the Mind

…If you continue in my word, then are you my disciples indeed; And you shall know the truth, and the truth shall make you free.

John 8:31-32

Satan tries to convince us that we are irredeemable or worthless, attempting to establish negative strongholds in our minds. Yet, we can win the battle of our minds by allowing God's truth to make us free.

Hardly anything is desired more than freedom. People die for it, pray for it and fight for it. We learn to resist Satan, to reject his lies by resisting them with truth, and learn to live free from fear and condemnation. We are valuable to Jesus and He loves us. His truth gives us the security and confidence we need. Real freedom comes from knowing truth.

Knowing truth is not simply something we ponder or believe. It becomes what we do, our way of life. Jesus often said in Scripture that we would be blessed if we did these things. Only by doing can we ever realize the truth that frees us. God has an appointed time for things, and when we put Him first, trust in His Word and timing, and maintain our faith, glorious things happen!

Day 173 Love Conquers Fear

There is no fear in love; but perfect love casts out fear: because fear has torment. He that fears is not made perfect in love.

I John 4:18

People experience various types of fear, which can hinder or stop them. Fear keeps us from accomplishing our goals and responsibilities, from speaking up when we should, from fulfilling God's calling, and from being the individuals He intends for us to be. Fear and faith are total opposites, and we will live a more enjoyable life if we live by faith rather than by fear.

Fear opens the door for Satan to torment us, while faith and love guides us into the holy manifest presence of Jesus, and in His "presence is fullness of joy" (Psalm 16:11). The best way to defeat fear is with the love of God. Today's Scripture reveals that love conquers fear! God's love gives us everything we need to do what we have been called to do. Fear has no influence over our lives if we are securely focused on the love of Jesus. His love drives out all fear!

We need love and faith to conquer life's burdens, pressures, and trials. Let us not lose another day guided by fear. Give all those fears to Jesus and rejoice in the wonderful life He has blessed us with—a life guided by faith and love. May we allow God's love to flood our hearts and minds and always remember, Jesus loves us with an everlasting love.

Day 174 Courage to Be Our Best

The Lord is my strength and my shield; my heart trusted in him, and I am helped: therefore my heart greatly rejoices; and with my song will I praise him.

Psalm 28:7

Trusting Jesus with our hearts so He can help us takes courage. Being transparent and vulnerable with Him and trusting Him with all areas of our lives that we find difficult to face is precisely what He wants from us. Jesus is the only one who can forgive, heal, and love us through each situation and provide the support we need.

Our God is Omnipotent and Omniscient. We can really do all things with Him and through Him. Having faith in Jesus allows Him to bring strength, security, help, and the ability to complete any task before us. We need to believe we can, rather than being afraid we cannot. We are stronger than we realize, because Christ is within and He will never leave nor forsake us. Knowing Jesus produces faith, hope, and courage.

True courage is never letting our actions be guided by our fears. It requires courage to be our best selves…so we can do our best work…so we can be the change we want to see…so we can do what God most needs us to do.

Day 175 Better is On the Way

Better is the end of a thing than the beginning thereof: and the patient in spirit is better than the proud in spirit.

Ecclesiastes 7:8

One major problem in today's society is that we seem to go from one thing to another, expecting everything to come to us quick and easy. We have difficulty enduring through problems and patiently waiting for a breakthrough. Jesus never hurries, quits, or becomes impatient. His love is patient, persistent, and persevering.

Spiritual growth is not like fast food. Instead, it requires time for its roots to develop, compelling us to be cooperative and patient. "In your patience possess you your souls" (Luke 21:19). Better is on the way, if we will patiently wait for it.

We must not prevent better from coming by dwelling on our past failures and regrets. Release all those past mistakes in prayer to Jesus and confidently await better. If our new beginning has not turned out as we expected, be encouraged. Better is on the way! "Better is the end of a thing…"

Day 176 Living in God's Pasture

Know you that the Lord he is God: it is he that has made us, and not we ourselves; we are his people, and the sheep of his pasture.

Psalm 100:3

God reminds us in this verse that everything was made by Him and belongs to Him. Sometimes we think we own everything around us. Jesus created everything, so He is in charge of it all. We are His people and we live in His pasture.

Desiring to be someone else is a waste of who we are. When we do not like ourselves, it is difficult to like anyone else. God's love for us enables us to accept ourselves as His creation and allows Him to guide us toward becoming the special and rare individuals He has destined us to be. Self-acceptance is key to living confidently, which is possible through deep faith in our Lord and trust in His plan for our lives. So we should stop comparing ourselves to others, yet value them for the individuals they are, and enjoy who we are! Finally, let us alter our focus from a "mine" mentality to rely on the true Owner of it all.

May we use what Jesus has blessed us with for His desires and less for our own. We are His people and the sheep of His pasture.

Day 177 Our Glorious Inheritance

In whom also we have obtained an inheritance, being predestinated according to the purpose of him who works all things after the counsel of his own will.

Ephesians 1:11

As a Christian, we have a spiritual inheritance. Life provides endless trials and tribulations, yet we can know what is duly ours by putting our faith and confidence in Jesus Christ.

We do not have to live our lives in an emotional and unstable whirlwind, feeling positive and upbeat one day and then negative and hopeless the next. In the place of instability we can live how God wants us to live, filled with peace, confidence, and being secure in knowing who we are in Jesus and realizing we belong to Him. What an amazing and glorious blessing! We are heirs to the Most High God! We do not receive His inheritance because we have a special last name or because we worked so hard and were ultimately noticed by Him. We receive this eternal inheritance because of the work Jesus did for us on Calvary's cross. Jesus wants to give us this inheritance, so he made it possible for us to receive it.

Let us claim our inheritance today! Be at peace, overflowing with love and happiness, and enjoy all we have in Jesus Christ. "For the kingdom of God is not meat and drink; but righteousness, and peace, and joy in the Holy Ghost" (Romans 14:17).

Day 178 Enjoy Life

And my soul shall be joyful in the Lord: it shall rejoice in his salvation.

Psalm 35:9

In today's Psalm, David realized the Lord's salvation for his life and rested in the blessed assurance that God would deliver him from his enemies who celebrated his failures and mocked him. David did not cower in fear of his enemies. Instead, he faced them with relentless determination to depend solely on the Most High God. David chose to rejoice in God's presence and salvation.

Realizing Jesus is with us, no matter what happens, we should be able to have joy in everything we do. As Christians, the world should be able to see us as the happiest people on Earth. Yet, numerous Christians walk around with negative and critical attitudes, displaying "sad-sack" faces. For every minute we complain, we lose sixty seconds of happiness. We are usually as happy as we determine in our minds to be. We choose our attitudes. Happiness is a choice. Positivity is a choice. Compassion is a choice. Generosity is a choice. Respect is a choice. Whatever we choose shapes us into who we are.

May we choose wisely and allow our rejoicing in Jesus to spread joy to others. One of the most effective and simplest ways to show Jesus to others is to smile and enjoy life.

Day 179 Joyful Awareness of His Presence

Surely you have granted him unending blessings and made him glad with the joy of your presence.

Psalm 21:6

Jesus wants us to experience joy in the midst of our normal daily lives, even on our worst days. Each day presents situations that could upset us, but we choose a positive attitude that honors Him, remaining peaceful and self-controlled. We allow God to use any difficulties to develop our character.

Regardless of what happens, we can be sure that Jesus is working everything out for our good. We should devote time right now to reflecting on the good things He has done in our lives. Consider the problems He has guided us through, the times He has healed us, and how wonderful it is to realize He cares for us and hears our prayers. The more time we spend intentionally seeking the Lord, the greater awareness we will experience of His presence. When we find joy in His presence, we are set on the path to living the abundant life that He desires for all His children.

May Jesus give us the fulness of peace and joy we need to love ourselves and others. When life brings storms, look for the rainbows.

Day 180 The Great God Living Within

You are of God, little children, and have overcome them: because greater is he that is in you, than he that is in the world.

I John 4:4

The way we overcome is not through carnal effort, but with the power and the love of Jesus living on the inside. This type of victory comes from God who is greater! He is greater than our problems, greater than our weaknesses, greater than anything! This means we never face difficult circumstances alone.

We have all we need to be successful and to be an overcomer. When we walk with Jesus, every day can be a wonderful day. We should not allow things around us to determine our quality of life. Our happiness is not predicated on what is occurring around us, but rather what is happening inside us. Jesus came to give us an abundant life (see John 10:10). God does not want us struggling to simply get through the day; but rather, He wants us to enjoy living! He wants us to live in abundant, overflowing joy every day!

Joy does not simply happen to us. We must choose joy daily. May we find joy in everything we choose to do…every job, relationship, and experience. Let us choose to lean on the Great One living in us. Our God is GREATER!

The End

www.ingramcontent.com/pod-product-compliance
Lightning Source LLC
La Vergne TN
LVHW052030170826
845678LV00018B/2199

* 9 7 9 8 7 3 9 6 8 5 1 4 8 *